Henry Purcell's *Dido and Aeneas*

Henry Purcell's
Dido and Aeneas

by

Ellen T. Harris

CLARENDON PRESS · OXFORD
1987

Oxford University Press, Walton Street, Oxford OX2 6DP
Oxford New York Toronto
Delhi Bombay Calcutta Madras Karachi
Petaling Jaya Singapore Hong Kong Tokyo
Nairobi Dar es Salaam Cape Town
Melbourne Auckland
and associated companies in
Beirut Berlin Ibadan Nicosia

Oxford is a trade mark of Oxford University Press

Published in the United States
by Oxford University Press, New York

British Library Cataloguing in Publication Data
Harris, Ellen T.
Henry Purcell's Dido and Aeneas.
1. Purcell, Henry. Dido and Aeneas
I. Title
782.1'092'4   ML410.P93
ISBN 0–19–315253–3

Library of Congress in Cataloguing in Publication Data
Harris, Ellen. T.
Henry Purcell's Dido and Aeneas.
Bibliography: p.
includes index.
1. Purcell, Henry, 1659–1695. Dido and Aeneas.
I. Title.
ML410.P93H3   1987   782.1'092'4   87–5621
ISBN 0–19–315253–3

Printed in Great Britain
at the University Printing House, Oxford
by David Stanford
Printer to the University

dedicated
to
Marian and Ann

Preface

My first association with Henry Purcell's *Dido and Aeneas* was as a singer. Initially I learned only Dido's lament, but gradually I came to know and love the entire opera. Much later, in the course of preparing and writing *Handel and the Pastoral Tradition*, I became fascinated with *Dido*'s historical position in Restoration theatre. Although many still view it as some sort of operatic anomaly, *Dido and Aeneas* is actually deeply rooted in English seventeenth-century theatrical and musical traditions. Most recently I prepared a new edition of the opera. This led me, of course, to a detailed study of the surviving sources. The background for this book, therefore, derives equally from my vocal, historical, and editorial interest in Purcell's remarkable opera. I only hope that in addition to whatever else the book offers about *Dido and Aeneas* that it succeeds in communicating my continued delight in and enthusiasm for it.

The book is organized so that it examines the history of *Dido*'s creation and critical reception in as close to chronological order as possible. Thus, Part I begins with a brief summary of the cultural climate in which *Dido* was written, including the contemporary musical and theatrical conventions. It then examines the choice of the subject and its classical and modern antecedents. Finally, the literary style of the finished libretto is analysed in light of English seventeenth-century discussions on how to write text for musical setting.

Part II focuses on the musical composition. It begins necessarily with an evaluation of the surviving musical sources, all of which post-date the opera's première by at least eighty years. A comparison of these scores with the original libretto raises questions about textual assignation (where the libretto and scores assign lines to different characters), scoring (where the libretto and scores conflict in their use of solo, ensemble, and choral pieces), structure (in terms of act and scene divisions), and use of dance. In discussing the differing designations for dances, an attempt has been made, as elsewhere, to distinguish carefully between the textual and musical sources. Thus, the dance that in the libretto is described as being led by the Jack of the Lanthorn becomes in the scores The Witches Dance. These are distinguished in the text as are the Eccho [*sic*] Dance of the Fairies and the Echo Dance of the Furies. Part II concludes with extensive chapters on musical declamation and ground bass composition.

Part III examines the performance history and critical reception of *Dido and Aeneas* from the late eighteenth-century adaptation for the Academy of Ancient Music to the nineteenth- and twentieth-century revivals that involved many of England's greatest vocal composers, including Gustav Holst, Ralph Vaughan Williams, Benjamin Britten, and Michael Tippett. The book concludes with a brief Appendix that offers an annotated, chronological list of the national premières of *Dido and Aeneas*, a historical survey of its editions, and a critical discography.

In the preparation of this book, I have incurred many debts. I would like first to thank the American Council of Learned Societies for a Fellowship Grant (1980–1) that allowed me to complete a first draft of this material. Many librarians at many institutions offered patient and invaluable help and advice; I would like to thank particularly the staffs at Regenstein Library (the University of Chicago), the British Library, the Bodleian Library, the Royal College of Music, the Royal Academy of Music, the Folger Library, Senate House (the University of London), New York Public Library, the Library of Congress, Cambridge University Library, and the Cheshire County Council. In addition, the British Library, the National Portrait Gallery (London), the Bodleian Library, and the Royal College of Music kindly granted permission for manuscripts, prints, and portraits in their collections to be reproduced here.

I am especially grateful to the following scholars of seventeenth-century music and theatre for reading all or portions of this book at various stages and offering suggestions and criticisms: Ellen Rosand, Suzanne Gossett, Katherine Rohrer, Curtis Price, and Laura Damuth. Each has had a critical impact on the final version printed here. Let me also take this opportunity to thank Howard Brown for making his library available to me. Finally, I must acknowledge an enormous debt to my research assistants, David Hurley and Joseph Auner, who not only typed this manuscript on disk and prepared it with Oxford coding, but also offered acute perceptions that have helped to clarify the argument in a number of passages.

My family, as always, was greatly supportive, especially considering that this book was in preparation over such a long period. I hope, at least, that my daughters will have learned the lesson offered to the Chelsea schoolgirls in the first performance of Purcell's *Dido and Aeneas*.

Contents

List of Plates

(between pages 68 and 69)

1. Portrait of Henry Purcell, attributed to Godfrey Kneller
   National Portrait Gallery

2. *Dido and Aeneas,* first page of 1689 libretto
   Royal College of Music

3. *Dido and Aeneas,* 1689 libretto, end of Act II
   Royal College of Music

4. *Dido and Aeneas,* Tenbury MS 1266, pp. 52–3, end of Act II
   Bodleian Library

5. *Measure for Measure,* 1700 playbook, masque, *The Loves of Dido and Aeneas*
   British Library

6. Academy of Ancient Music, programme for 22 February 1787
   Royal College of Music

7. *Dido and Aeneas,* Academy version
   British Library, Add. MS 31540

8. 'Ah, Belinda', from *Orpheus Britannicus,* 1698
   British Library

9. Portrait of Henry Purcell by John Closterman
   National Portrait Gallery

Part I

Background to the Music

Introduction to Part I

Henry Purcell's *Dido and Aeneas* stands as the greatest operatic achievement of the English seventeenth century. Although it lacks the monumental dimensions of a Wagnerian opera, for the opera was originally composed not for the public theatre, but for a private girls' school in Chelsea and takes little more than an hour to perform, Purcell's composition withstands comparison with operatic works from any period for its ability to express human passion in a perfect blend of words and music. The achievement, however, was not Purcell's alone. Partly he was lucky in the choice of subject—for the story of a woman loved and left by a foreign military officer is one that transcends the boundaries of time, as can be seen in the earlier seventeenth-century popularity of the legend of Ariadne and Theseus, as well as in the sustained success of such nineteenth-century operas as Delibes' *Lakmé* and Puccini's *Madama Butterfly*. Even more, Purcell was lucky in his librettist, Nahum Tate, a poet of modest talents and infamous for his happy ending to Shakespeare's *King Lear*, who was able to create a libretto beautifully suited to musical setting and enhancement.

The choice of the subject and the writing of the libretto, as well as contemporary cultural trends and the planned performance at a girls' school, were factors that preceded and influenced the composition of the music. In Part I the preconditions of the music will be examined in three sections: (1) the history of the first performance and the cultural fashions of the time, (2) the story, its literary antecedents and relation to seventeenth-century dramatic traditions, and (3) the style of the libretto in light of contemporary conventions.

I

First Performance:
Place, Date, and Artistic Climate

The most obvious question about an opera's first performance—when?—has been for *Dido* the hardest to answer. The first page of the single surviving libretto (shown in Plate 2) describes the work fully as

> An Opera, Perform'd at Mr. Josias Priest's Boarding-School at Chelsey. By Young Gentlewomen. The Words by Mr. Nat. Tate. The Musick Compos'd by Mr. Purcell.[1]

The information offered is quite precise, giving author, composer, and place of performance, and telling us further that the opera was performed privately and by amateurs. The libretto only lacks a date.

Dido and Aeneas was first discussed in print by Sir John Hawkins in his *General History of the Science and Practice of Music* (1776), where he writes,

> One Josias Priest, a celebrated dancing-master and a composer of stage dances, kept a boarding school for young gentlewomen in Leicester Fields. The nature of his profession inclining him to dramatic representation, he got Tate to write, and Purcell to set to music, a little drama, called 'Dido and Aeneas'. Purcell was then of the Age of nineteen . . .[2]

This passage placed the opera in 1677 as Purcell's first theatrical effort. No reason is given, but W. Barclay Squire has surmised,

---

[1] A single copy of the libretto is preserved at the Royal College of Music, London.
[2] Sir John Hawkins, *A General History of the Science and Practice of Music* (London: Novello, Elver & Co., 1875), ii, 745. (The original edition of this history was published 1776.)

4

undoubtedly correctly, that Hawkins knew of Tate's play *Brutus of Alba* (1678), which also tells the story of Aeneas and Dido, but in different guise.[3] In the preface to the play Tate writes, 'I had begun and finisht it under the names of *Dido and Aeneas*', and, as Barclay Squire puts it, 'Hawkins probably inferred from this that Purcell's libretto was the first version of Tate's play, and he fixed the date at 1677 . . .' Hawkins, however, gives Leicester Fields as the place of performance, not Chelsea, as in the libretto. And in the mid-nineteenth century, when the libretto first came to light, this discrepancy led to a new dating, for an advertisement in the *London Gazette* of November 22–5, 1680, states that '*Josias Priest*, Dancing-Master, who kept a Boarding-School of Gentlewomen in *Leicester Fields*, is removed to the great School-House at Chelsea'. Thus, not to conflict with the libretto, the date was altered to 1680, and there the matter stood until the early twentieth century.

Noting that the Epilogue to *Dido* was published in Thomas D'Urfey's *New Poems* of 1690, and that it had not appeared in that poet's collection of 1683, Barclay Squire argued that the date of *Dido* must be later than 1680. He also pointed to the content of the Epilogue, which seems to refer directly to the revolution of 1688. This and biographical evidence about D'Urfey, as well as the maturity of the opera's musical style, led him to redate the opera to 1689.

Since Barclay Squire's work, the only contributions to the dating of *Dido* have been attempts to determine the exact month of composition. Grattan Flood (1918) placed it in December, based on biographical evidence about the reader of the Epilogue, Lady Dorothy Burke.[4] John Buttrey (1967), noting that, although the date of publication for D'Urfey's poems is 1690, the volume appeared in November 1689, associated the first performance with the birthday of Queen Mary (30 April), a deduction based primarily on the paean to spring with which the opera's Prologue ends.[5] And finally, Margaret Laurie (1979), pointing to the allegorical beginning of the Prologue that depicts the accession of

[3] W. Barclay Squire, 'Purcell's *Dido and Aeneas*', *The Musical Times*, liv (1918), 253. The remainder of this paragraph derives also from this article.

[4] W. H. Grattan Flood, 'Purcell's *Dido and Aeneas*: Who was Lady Dorothy Burke?', *The Musical Times*, liv (1918), 515.

[5] John Buttrey, 'Dating Purcell's *Dido and Aeneas*', *Proceedings of the Royal Music Association*, xciv (1967–8), 51–62.

William and Mary, places the opera at the time of their corona-
tion (21 April 1689).[6]

There is not much to choose between the theories of Buttrey
and Laurie (nine days, to be exact), but Laurie probably has
identified the occasion correctly, since a birthday ode by Purcell
does exist that has been dated to 1689—'Now does the glorious
day appear'. But April 1689 is certainly specific enough, so that it
is finally possible to place *Dido and Aeneas* properly within
Purcell's lifetime and in relation to his theatrical works.

In his brief life of thirty-six years (1659–95), Purcell was known
best for his dramatic stage works, as he is still today. His
contributions to that medium began in 1680 with incidental
music for Nathaniel Lee's *Theodosius*, and thereafter his music
appeared with increasing regularity. Between 1680 and 1688
Purcell wrote music for seven plays. His eighth score followed in
1689, the year of *Dido*, and by the time of his death six years later,
Purcell had contributed music to forty-three plays in all.[7] The
music for these, however, can hardly be called dramatic, even
though it is sometimes placed very effectively within the spoken
drama. That is, the instrumental movements and individual songs
generally are dramatic because of their use within the play and not
because of their musical content. *Dido and Aeneas* thus gave
Purcell his first chance to write a sustained musical setting of a
dramatic text, and it was his only opportunity to compose a work
in which the music carried the entire drama. It is Purcell's only
opera in the modern sense of the term.

In Restoration England, musical entertainments normally con-
sisted of a spoken play with extensive musical interludes more or
less attached to the plot. John Dryden, the leading Restoration
playwright, dubbed these works 'dramatic operas', while Roger
North, a contemporary amateur musician and critic, called them
'semi-operas'.[8] In 1685 Dryden defined the genre as,

> A tragedy mixed with opera or a drama written in blank verse,
> adorned with scenes, machines, songs and dances, so that the fable

---

[6] Margaret Laurie, ed., *Dido and Aeneas* (London: New Purcell Society Edition, 1979),
Preface, ix.

[7] The statistics here and below concerning Purcell's compositions have been derived
from the work lists in Franklin B. Zimmerman, *Henry Purcell (1659–1695): An Analytical
Catalogue of his Music* (London: Macmillan, 1963).

[8] Roger North, *Memoirs of Music*, ed. Edward F. Rimbault (London, 1846), 115 ff.

of it is all spoken and acted by the best of the comedians, the other part of the entertainment to be performed by ... singers and dancers ... It cannot properly be called a play, because the action of it is supposed to be conducted sometimes by supernatural means or magic, nor an opera, because the story of it is not sung.[9]

Between 1690 and his death in 1695, Purcell composed the music for five dramatic operas: *Dioclesian* (1690, based on a play by Fletcher, *The Prophetess*), *King Arthur* (1691, with a text by Dryden), *The Fairy Queen* (1692, an adaptation of Shakespeare's *A Midsummer Night's Dream*), *The Indian Queen* (1695, also by Dryden), and *Timon of Athens* (1694, adapted from Shakespeare).[10]

Dido stands apart from this group in size as well as content. It is conceived on a small scale for what must have been a small, private audience. It is short and demands less in the way of vocal technique than the later works, and its orchestra consists only of strings, whereas the dramatic operas include beautiful and effective writing for woodwinds and trumpet. Nevertheless, from our historical vantage point, *Dido and Aeneas* is the most progressive of Purcell's stage works. Unlike the music for the stage plays or the dramatic operas, *Dido and Aeneas* offers a complete drama set to music. Thus it deals not simply with human emotions, as do many of the songs of the other stage works, but it shows these developing in specific characters over the course of the action. In the plays and dramatic operas the main characters rarely, if ever, sing, and the music in both remains largely incidental to the dramatic action. For these reasons *Dido* holds our attention on today's stage, whereas the more lavish dramatic operas are mostly unknown except in concert versions of the music. Purcell's opera was not, however, a unique phenomenon in this period; it represents rather a culminating point in a lively, if undernourished, tradition of its own.

Dido and Aeneas derives from the seventeenth-century English masque tradition. It is beholden most obviously to its immediate predecessor, *Venus and Adonis* (c.1685) by John Blow, Purcell's

---

[9] John Dryden, Preface to *Albion and Albanius* (1685) in *Essays of John Dryden*, ed. W. P. Ker (Oxford: Oxford University Press, 1926) i, 278.

[10] The incidental music from *The Tempest* once attributed to Purcell is now thought to be by John Weldon. See Margaret Laurie, 'Did Purcell set the *Tempest*?', *Proceedings of the Royal Music Association*, xc (1963–4), 43–57.

teacher and friend. This masque in turn was based on a tradition that can be traced back to Matthew Locke's *Cupid and Death* (1653/9), to the pre-Commonwealth masques of William and Henry Lawes (especially the musically continuous sections of *The Triumph of Peace*, 1633, by William, text by James Shirley; and the dramatically coherent *Comus*, 1634, by Henry, text by John Milton), and the masque developments begun by Ben Jonson during the reign of James I. This tradition can be described as one that sought dramatically to distil the diverse and entertaining elements of the court masque, including spectacle, dance, poetry, and music, into a unified plot, and musically to seek an effective way to compose dramatic declamation.

If drama and music had been allowed to develop in this direction, an English opera, modelled no doubt on Italian conventions, could have resulted. But the pre-Commonwealth royalty preferred spectacle to dramatic continuity, and in the battle between playwright Ben Jonson and scenic designer Inigo Jones, the outcome was decided by Charles I: Jones was the decisive winner, Jonson being relieved of the responsibility of writing texts for the court masque. Thus the Stuart masques began to move further and further away from continuous drama as they embraced an episodic structure that allowed for as many scenes and machines as possible.

Meanwhile the popularity of the masque had resulted in its transference to the public stage where masque-like entertainments were inserted into plays. With the demise of the court masque after the Commonwealth this stage tradition was expanded, and the Restoration theatre took over the use of spectacular devices in large and elaborate masque interpolations. However, the strong literary tradition of Shakespeare, Fletcher, and Jonson (playwrights in whose works the theatre masques first appeared), which was inherited and revived at the hands of Restoration dramatists such as Dryden, stood in the way of music gaining a larger role in the drama. And thus Dramatic Opera was born. It should be remembered that three of Purcell's five such works were based on plays by Shakespeare or Fletcher; two were newly written by Dryden.

It is no surprise, then, that when the first public performance of *Dido* took place the opera was broken up into four sections as musical episodes in a play. This occurred in 1700, five years after Purcell's death, in Charles Gildon's adaptation of Shakespeare's

Measure for Measure (see Plate 5). The playbook shows that the material from *Dido* was sometimes taken out of order, altered, and expanded. In 1704 *Dido* reappeared, apparently in the right order and complete, but now as a musical Epilogue to two different plays—this being an accepted way of including all-sung operas on an evening's programme. In fact, such was the English aversion to a full evening's entertainment of musically continuous opera that even the first Italian opera performed in eighteenth-century London, *Arsinoe* of 1705, was cut, translated into English, and 'introduced' by a one-act spoken play.[11]

While the strength of the spoken theatre on the public stage kept music in a role of dramatic device or incidental decoration, masque-like compositions allowing for music throughout, or throughout substantial portions, were written for private occasions, just as *Dido* was written for a girls' school. Their relative obscurity can be attributed directly to the contemporary taste for dramatic opera rather than for such compositions. Thus there is no need to wonder that Purcell's contemporaries took so little notice of his only opera. It has already been mentioned that in musical style and orchestration *Dido* is simpler than Purcell's later compositions; it also lacks scenic displays and stage machinery. These seeming deficiencies, however, did not entirely prevent the opera from being noticed, as its inclusion in *Measure for Measure* indicates. Put simply, all-sung operas were not what held the stage in Restoration England, but when combined with a play, *Dido* became acceptable. In the decade before *Dido*, Matthew Locke had written of his dramatic opera *Psyche* that 'the author prudently considered that, though Italy was and is the great academy of the world for that science of through-composed opera, England is not, and therefore mixed it with interlocutions as more proper to our genius.'[12] In 1692, shortly after *Dido*, the popular librettist Pierre Motteux wrote, 'Experience hath taught us that our English genius will not relish that perpetual singing.'[13]

[11] Curtis Price, *Music in the Restoration Theatre* (Ann Arbor, Mich.: UMI, 1979), 114–15. The first Italian opera performed in London was probably Cavalli's *Erismena*, translated into English and performed in London in 1674; see Eric Walter White, 'English Opera Research—The Immediate Past and the Future: A Personal Viewpoint', *Theatre Notebook*, xxi (1966), 34.

[12] As quoted in Dennis Arundell, *The Critic at the Opera* (London, 1957), 123.

[13] As quoted from *The Gentleman's Journal* (Jan. 1692) in Robert Etheridge Moore, *Henry Purcell and the Restoration Theatre* (Cambridge, Mass.: Harvard University Press, 1961), 33.

The simple beauty of the music, the directness of the plot, and the passionate expression of human emotion, therefore, were not in themselves sufficient to override the strong theatrical traditions of the time. Nevertheless, the success of *Dido*'s composition is probably what led to the requests for Purcell's music in the larger 'operas' for the public stage, for Purcell's dramatic operas all post-date 1689. In this sense, then, *Dido* was neither unimportant nor obscure; it was Purcell's moment of recognition in the theatrical community. In the nine years before *Dido* Purcell composed incidental music for seven plays. In the six years following *Dido* he wrote incidental music for thirty-five plays and for five dramatic operas.

2

Text: Synopsis and History

The story of *Dido and Aeneas* derives from the original source in Virgil's epic the *Aeneid*, and the basic outlines of the plot are probably familiar to most readers. Aeneas leaves the destroyed city of Troy with a band of devoted followers; their object is to found a new state in Italy. After seven tempest-tossed years the ragged and diminished fleet takes harbour at the city of Carthage where the widowed queen Dido welcomes them with warm hospitality. Although Dido and Aeneas fall in love, Dido resists her emotions because of the vow of chastity she swore after her husband's death and her fears about Aeneas's fidelity. Indeed, Dido has previously turned down an offer of marriage from Iarbas, a neighbouring king. Dido's relationship with Aeneas, however, develops with the aid of supportive goddesses—Dido has Juno, and Aeneas, his mother, Venus. Although in opposition on most matters, the goddesses agree (each with the hope of improving the happiness or situation of her ward) to hasten the union. Thus to weaken Dido's resolve Venus sends Cupid and disguises him in the form of Ascanius, Aeneas's young son whom Dido keeps with her in the palace, and Juno conjures up a storm during a hunting party so that Dido and Aeneas must take shelter in a cave. Here their love is consummated. Consequently Aeneas devotes himself entirely to his mistress, but Jove, discovering Aeneas's dalliance, sends Mercury to remind the hero of his destiny to found a kingdom at Rome. Aeneas, though stunned by this message, accepts it immediately, and his sorrow at leaving Dido is more than matched by his resolve to go. Dido pleads, threatens, and begs to no avail. After Aeneas departs, she kills herself on his sword.

Tate's libretto makes a number of basic changes in this outline. The number of characters is reduced, and the mythological figures are replaced by witches who successfully plot Dido's fall. Dido, however, is not tricked into her relationship with Aeneas,

11

as happens in the *Aeneid*, and she dies a natural (not violent) death
from grief. In its broad outline, however, the story is basically
familiar.[14]

The opera opens at the Carthaginian court. Belinda, an attendant lady who replaces Dido's sister Anna of Virgil's narrative,
guesses the reason for her mistress's evident unhappiness and
jauntily tells her not to worry over imagined difficulties. The
courtiers quickly agree. Nevertheless, Dido remains aloof and
refuses to speak of the source of her torment. Belinda perseveres
in her efforts and verbalizes Dido's hidden passion, after which a
second unnamed lady, called simply the Second Woman, urges a
union to strengthen the security of Carthage. Again the courtiers
concur. This encouragement gives Dido the freedom to reveal her
love, but she is uninterested in its political implications. Rather,
she enumerates Aeneas's personal attributes—his virtue, his prow-
ess, his courage, and his charm. When Belinda and the Second
Woman admit the strong allure of such traits, Dido confesses her
fear that she will be overwhelmed.

Belinda and the other lady now rush in with the second line of
encouragement. They have presumably expressed their deepest
concerns first—a hope for greater political security—but now
they turn to Dido's own needs and tell her that Aeneas suffers
from love every bit as much as she. This sentiment is repeated
exactly by all the courtiers. Aeneas then enters for the first time,
and Belinda comments to her Queen on his 'godlike' appearance.
He wastes no time in taking up the previous arguments and pleads
with Dido to release him from love's anguish and political
insecurity. Dido reminds Aeneas of his destiny, which he vows to
defy, and the courtiers comment on how lovesick the warrior has
become. Aeneas then resumes the double plea for empire and
passion, and his pathetic stance leads Belinda to offer him
encouragement.

More and more Dido shows signs of relenting, and the
courtiers proclaim the 'triumphs of love and of beauty' to 'the
hills and the vales'. A celebratory dance follows. Although Tate
allows for no explicit love scene, perhaps with a regard for the
young gentlewomen of the Chelsea boarding school, it must be

---

[14] The textual summary that follows is based in part on the text in the musical sources.
For a discussion of the differences between the texts of the libretto and the later musical
scores, see below, Part II.

assumed by the end of this scene that Dido, besieged from within and without, has succumbed to the strength of her own passion.

The scene changes to a darkened cave, where the Sorceress calls up her attendants for help in 'a mischief'. They enter hurriedly with the glee of anticipation. After the Sorceress states her intention to deprive Dido 'of fame, of life, and love', they ask, 'How shall this be done?' The Sorceress explains that after Dido and Aeneas return from the hunt, sounds of which now penetrate to the cave, she plans to deceive Aeneas with a conjured vision of Mercury commanding him to pursue his fate by immediately departing from Carthage. This delicious plot elicits more laughter from the attendants, and two witches add to the general glee with a decision 'to mar their hunting sport' with a storm. A somberness then settles over the group as it turns to perform the evil rites. An 'Eccho dance of the Inchantresses and Fairies' concludes the scene.

The next scene opens upon the grove where the hunt is drawing to a close. Belinda leads the chorus in a song praising both the sport and the surroundings. The omens, however, portend ill. Belinda sings of the presence of Diana—goddess of the hunt, to be sure, but also goddess of chastity, an attribute that Dido has just lost. When the Second Woman continues with a song to entertain the hunting party, she takes the reference to Diana and describes how in such groves 'Actaeon met his fate' and died because he invaded the goddess's privacy. And when Aeneas points to the excellence of the catch, he alludes to Venus and Adonis, a couple whose great love affair ended only after Adonis was mortally wounded during such a hunt.

Suddenly the skies darken, and thunder rolls. Dido urges everyone to hurry back to town, and the cry is quickly taken up by all as they collect their belongings and rush out. As Aeneas starts off, however, he is detained by the false Mercury. The warrior accepts the apparently heaven-sent edict, but is then troubled by Dido's reaction and, finally, by his own conflicting emotions. As in the stories of Actaeon and of Venus and Adonis, a seemingly innocent hunting party will soon lead to loss of love and life.

The next scene changes to one in which the sailors, watched over by the exultant witches, are happily preparing the ships for their departure. The Sorceress, at the height of her powers, now makes plans to continue harassing Aeneas with storms at sea once he embarks, and the witches revel in their success, laughing all the while. The scene closes with a dance.

The setting of the final scene is not immediately clear; it may still be at the port or perhaps at the palace. Evidently Dido and Belinda have been arguing about Dido's next course of action, having seen that the Trojan ships are being readied for departure, and it seems Belinda has continued to urge Aeneas on her mistress. Dido, however, resolutely rejects such advice. As Aeneas enters Belinda hesitantly attempts once again to persuade her mistress of his fidelity, but she is silenced by the ensuing confrontation between the lovers. While Aeneas appears crushed by his destiny, Dido now behaves in truly regal fashion. After calling him hypocritical for blaming heaven rather than owning up to his own actions, she abruptly orders him to leave. When he begs to be allowed to stay, she threatens to kill herself, and he departs. Only then does Dido admit she must die nevertheless. The courtiers comment that 'great minds against themselves conspire', after which Dido appears already to be dying. She asks for Belinda's hand and prays that her sins will not trouble Belinda after she is gone. Her last wish is that Belinda remember her but forget her fate. The courtiers conclude the opera with a chorus of mourning.

A comparison of Tate's libretto and Book IV of Virgil's *Aeneid* reveals that Tate's two basic changes, the substitution of witches for goddesses and the non-violent death of Dido, lead to funda-mental changes in the characterization of the lovers. It is clear that Dido, pressured by her friends and pursued by Aeneas, is finally seduced by Aeneas against her better judgement. Here there are no meddling goddesses to plot and prepare the union. In *Dido and Aeneas* Dido alone must take responsibility for her fall from chastity. This she does, for if her passions have tormented her and made her weak, Aeneas's infidelity gives her strength.

On the other hand, Aeneas, in this version, plays the fool. Not for him the heaven-sent messenger but instead a conjured illusion. He has pleaded with Dido for her love and sworn to forego his destiny ('let Dido smile and I'll defy the feeble stroke of Destiny'), but faced with an ephemera he instantly recants and blames the gods ('yours be the blame ye gods') rather than his own weakness. Dido chides him for it ('thus hypocrites that murder act / make heaven and gods the authors of the fact'), and only then does he offer to stay; but it is too late. Aeneas leaves a broken man, and Dido suffers a spiritually induced·death (there is no sword, no suicide). Her last words do not mention Aeneas, only her 'wrongs' and her 'fate'.

How different is Virgil's couple! They are essentially the puppets of the gods, and thus no questions arise as to their responsibility. Dido's submission only takes place through manipulation by two goddesses, and Aeneas is truly visited by Jove's messenger, Mercury. The hero never swears to defy his destiny and thus never breaks his promise. The moment that Dido succumbs, a moment lacking in Tate's adaptation, is vividly described by Virgil (IV, 165–72):

> Now Dido and the prince Aeneas found themselves
> In the same cave. Primordial Earth and presiding Juno
> Gave the signal. The firmament flickered with fire, a witness
> Of wedding. Somewhere above, the Nymphs cried out in
>   pleasure.
> That day was doom's first birthday and that first day was the
>   cause of
> Evils: Dido recked nothing for appearance or reputation:
> The love she brooded on now was a secret love no longer;
> Marriage, she called it, drawing the word to veil her sin.[15]

After deciding to leave, Aeneas speaks roughly to the Queen of their relationship (IV, 333–42; 345–7).

>   Dido, I'll never pretend
> You have not been good to me, deserving of everything
> You can claim. I shall not regret my memories of Elissa[16]
> As long as I breathe, as long as I remember my own self.
> For my conduct—this, briefly: I did not look to make off from
>   here
> In secret—do not suppose it; nor did I offer you marriage
> At any time or consent to be bound by a marriage contract.

---

[15] This and all quotations from Virgil's *Aeneid* are taken from the verse translation by C. Day Lewis (London: Oxford University Press, 1952).

[16] Dido's first name was Elissa, meaning divine woman, and she is sometimes called this by both Virgil and Tate. She adopted the name Dido, meaning bold woman, after the death of her husband and the founding of Carthage.

If fate allowed me to be my own master, and gave me
Free will to choose my way of life, to solve my problems,
Old Troy would be my first choice . . .

      ·   ·   ·   ·   ·   ·   ·

            . . . But now Apollo and the Lycian
Oracle have told me that Italy is our bourne.
There lies my heart, my homeland.

Later Aeneas is compared to a 'stalwart oak-tree . . . assaulted
by a wintry wind whose veering gusts tear at it, trying to root it
up', and Dido, symbolized by this wind, rages wildly (IV, 600–2;
615–21):

Why could I not have seized him, torn up his body and littered
The sea with it? finished his friends with the sword, finished his
    own
Ascanius and served him up for his father to banquet on?

   ·   ·   ·   ·   ·   ·   ·

May he be harried in war by adventurous tribes, and exiled
From his own land; may Ascanius be torn from his arms; may
    he have to
Sue for aid, and see his own friends squalidly dying.
Yes, and when he's accepted the terms of a harsh peace,
Let him never enjoy his realm or the alloted span
But fall before his time and lie on the sands, unburied.
That is my last prayer. I pour it out, with my lifeblood.

Virgil's Dido then takes her own life, throwing herself on a
funeral pyre. Her final words ring out a curse upon her betrayer
(IV, 661–2):

May he look long, from out there on the deep, at my flaming
    pyre,
The heartless! And may my death-fires signal bad luck for his
    voyage!

The differences in characterization between the couples of
Virgil's and Tate's versions point, first, to the place where
Purcell's opera was originally performed—a girls' boarding
school. In Tate's libretto, morality and the moral replace both the
pleasure and pain of love. No nymphs cry out, and only a single

line of Aeneas's reveals that any pleasure has been enjoyed—and that brief; thinking of Dido's reaction to his departure, he moans,

> How can so hard a fate be took,
> One night enjoy'd, the next forsook.

Compare this to the rumour-mongering in Virgil (IV, 193–4):

> The couple are spending the winter in debauchery, the whole long Winter, forgetting their kingdoms, rapt in a trance of lust.

In Tate's libretto, Dido suffers for a single indiscretion, losing her reputation, love, and life, just as the Sorceress had predicted. She does not become crazed with rage or lovesickness. She does not beg Aeneas to stay; ultimately, she even orders him to go. She does not do violence to herself, but simply expires. The moral, of course, is that young girls should not accept the advances of young men no matter how ardent their wooing or how persistent their promises. Perhaps this is best expressed in the blatant callousness of the departing sailors:

> Take a boozy short leave of your nymphs on the shore,
> And silence their mourning with vows of returning,
> But never intending to visit them more.

Dido suffers the ultimate punishment for her sin. And it should be remembered that suicide is not a punishment, but a sin worse than sexual licence. Dido's life, like her love and reputation, is taken from her, and she dies. She is not a seductress or an evil enchantress who delays Aeneas's greater mission. Rather, it is Aeneas who is the villain, who, by being thoughtless and irresponsible, causes Dido's death. Both Curtis Price and John Buttrey have recently argued that Tate's libretto is but a thinly veiled allegory representing the contemporary English political situation.[17] Although there is reason for such an interpretation, especially in the text of the Prologue, the story of *Dido and Aeneas* and the place of its performance argue more forcibly for a reading

---

[17] Buttrey, 'Dating Purcell's *Dido and Aeneas*', and Curtis Price, *Henry Purcell and the London Stage* (Cambridge: Cambridge University Press, 1984).

as a morality. The allegorical interpretations, however, and the relevant contemporary political circumstances deserve discussion.

James II's open avowal of Catholicism was unpopular with English Protestants, who feared he might follow the French lead in declaring Protestantism heretical. William, Prince of Orange, Protestant grandson of Charles I of England and husband of Mary, daughter of James I by a first marriage, was called upon to challenge the throne. As he and his army arrived from Holland, James II and his family fled to France. Parliament thereupon agreed to allow William and Mary to reign together equally as monarchs. Even this situation, however, was seen by many to be less than ideal, for there was concern about having a 'foreign' king. In his interpretation, Buttrey emphasizes the fears of the English public about the joint sovereignty. Price, on the other hand, focuses on the Protestants' worries about Catholicism.

The Prologue, for which no music survives, begins with the direction: 'Phoebus Rises in the Chariot, Over the Sea', and the chorus pays tribute 'To the New rising Star of the Ocean'. Buttrey views this as 'an allusion to William's Channel-crossing'.[18] Then 'Venus Descends in her Chariot' and a Nereid and Phoebus discuss her arrival.

> NEREID. Look down ye Orbs and See
> A New Divinity.
> PHOEBUS. Whose Lustre does Out-Shine
> Your fainter Beams, and half Eclipses mine . . .

Buttrey describes this as 'a reference to the equal division of the monarchy'.[19] The rest of the Prologue is devoted mostly to singing the praises of Phoebus and Venus and of spring.

That the Prologue extols the virtues of the new King and Queen, especially considering that the opera was probably written, as Laurie believes, on the occasion of their accession to the throne, cannot be seriously doubted. What is difficult to accept is Buttrey's assertion that the rest of the opera is also a political allegory 'pointing out . . . the possible fate of the British nation should Dutch William fail in his responsibilities to his English queen.'[20] Such an allegory would have been grossly insulting to both William and Mary and particularly odd after the praise lavished on them during the Prologue. As Price has written, 'The

---

[18] Buttrey, 61.   [19] Ibid.   [20] Ibid., 60.

story of a prince who seduces and abandons a neurotic queen would seem a tactless way to honour the new monarchs.'[21] Nevertheless, Price also argues for an allegorical interpretation.

Recognizing the difficulties with Buttrey's analysis, Price admits that Tate 'was forced to adapt the Classical tale . . . to disengage Queen Mary from a symbolic link with Queen Dido'.[22] In his interpretation, 'the witches in *Dido* symbolize a new popish plot', a Catholic threat to undermine the joint sovereignty of William and Mary and re-establish James II on the throne.[23] Thus Dido and Aeneas both become victims of the witches, and 'Tate is forced to suppress Dido's faults in favour of a noble, almost austere righteousness.'[24] The most difficult stumbling block, of course, is Dido's death, and Price argues that Tate's decision was to leave the heroine lingering on the point of death but still alive.

The allegorical readings of both Buttrey and Price would have been offensive and disturbing to seventeenth-century audiences, and Price sees this as one reason *Dido* was never given a public performance in Purcell's lifetime. He argues that Buttrey's reading would have been 'the epitome of bad taste', and even if the Queen 'were left to linger on the point of death during her lover's "absence"', a production would still have been difficult during the 1690s when 'the king's absences became more frequent and protracted' and 'after Mary's death in 1694 it would have been unthinkable'.[25] Nevertheless, Price attributes the 'ultimate blame for the initial obscurity' of the opera not to the libretto but to Purcell himself, because, according to Price, he restores through his music what Tate had eliminated—Dido's 'obsessions, neuroses, even sexual desire', and finally her death. The contemporary lack of public enthusiasm for all-sung opera, however, makes this rather strained argument unnecessary.

Except for the allegorical Prologue, which was appropriately altered for the production in 1700 after Mary's death and eliminated in 1704 after William's death (see Part II below), it is difficult to countenance any theory of political allegory in *Dido*. Although it is certainly true that the story of Dido and Aeneas had previously served for political allegory especially during the reign of Elizabeth I, this does not make an allegorical reading of Tate's libretto or Purcell's score either more or less likely. At the very

---

[21] Price, 229. [23] Ibid., 233. [25] Ibid., 262.

[22] Ibid., 230. [24] Ibid.

least, these allegorical readings undervalue the relationship of the opera to Tate's play *Brutus of Alba*, which was written long before William and Mary took the throne.

Tate had faced the problem of making an evening's entertainment out of an episode in Virgil's epic many years before he had to consider creating a drama suitable for performance at a girls' boarding school. His first play, *Brutus of Alba*, appeared eleven years before *Dido* in 1678. In the preface Tate explains the source of its plot.[26]

> I wou'd not have the reader surpriz'd to find this Tragedy bear some Resemblance with the passages of the Fourth Book of the *Aeneids*, for I had begun and finisht it under the Name of *Dido and Aeneas*; but was wrought by the advice of some Friends, to Transform it to the Dress it now wears. They told me it wou'd appear Arrogant to attempt any Characters that had been written by the Incomparable Virgil; and therefore (though sensible enough of what I should lose by the Change) I chose to suffer any Inconvenience rather than be guilty of a breach of Modesty.

Tate's 'transformation' simply involved changing the main characters' names to the parallel figures in the accepted although mythical history of England presented by Geoffrey of Monmouth in the twelfth century. Aeneas thus becomes Brutus of Alba, and Dido, the Queen of Syracuse. In addition, Aeneas's son Ascanius is grown into a youth and named Locrinus, and the neighbouring monarch whose prior suit was rejected by the Queen (Dido) becomes the Agrigentine King, who like his model, Virgil's King Iarbus, is spoken about but never appears in person. The changes of name, however, make little difference to the well-known plot, and eleven years later, when Tate wrote the libretto for Purcell's opera, he shed his youthful, false modesty and returned the rightful names to the leading protagonists.

There are, as one might assume, many points of contact between these two dramas by Tate. The changes in characterization from Virgil's epic noted in the opera, for example, are already clearly apparent in the play; they simply reflect the changes in character motivation necessary for the refashioning of

---

[26] An original copy of the playbook (London, 1678) is preserved in Special Collections of Regenstein Library, University of Chicago.

an episode into a complete entity. In the *Aeneid* Aeneas and Dido
are manipulated by the gods and simply play out their assigned
roles in history. Tate, however, needed to eliminate such long-
range goals from his dramas.

Thus Tate substitutes witches for the mythological machinery
of Virgil. Whereas Venus aimed at giving Aeneas pleasure, and
Juno hoped to win Dido the empire meant for Aeneas, the
witches' motives are jealousy and envy. The goddesses had hoped
for good from their intervention, but had failed in the long run.
The witches desire the destruction of the Queen and succeed. In
Brutus, the sorceress Ragusa hears the sounds of the hunt and
exclaims,

> So merry!—Well, 'tis odds I marr your sport,
> By Contract, son, I hate all humane kind,
> But envy most the prosperous and great;
> Thou art devoted to the Queen's destruction,
> And so am I: this day begins the Ruine.

> (Act III)

In the parallel passage from the libretto the Sorceress tells her
attendants,

> The Queen of Carthage whom we hate,
> As we do all in prosp'rous state,
> Ere sunset shall most wretched prove.

And later, when the hunt is heard in the distance, two witches
exclaim,

> We'll conjure for a storm
> To mar their hunting sport.

The resemblances in wording are clear, but the important fact is
that in both cases the motivations of the Sorceresses do not exceed
beyond the boundaries of the play.

Of course, it would have been theoretically possible to devise a
different substitution for the mythological machinery than
witches, which could still have functioned within the confines of
the play. For example, Dido might have had a political rival who
took advantage of her love for Aeneas and used scheming and

disguises to cause her downfall. However, the witches not only maintain the aura of supernatural that belongs to mythology, but they were popular additions to seventeenth-century drama. Shakespeare's *Macbeth* (*c.*1609), where the witches are named 'Weird Sisters' as opposed to Tate's 'Wayward Sisters', was expanded with musical additions from Thomas Middleton's *The Witch* (1614), and during the Restoration the many revivals of *Macbeth* only further expanded the witches' music. Curtis Price points out the similarities of wording between William Davenant's adaptation of *Macbeth* (1661) and Tate's libretto, and he also documents similarities to Thomas Shadwell's play *The Lancashire Witches* (1681).[27] However, he plays down the importance of these resemblances, probably because they serve to diminish the possibility that Tate intended these characters as an allegorical representation of a popish plot, a role they certainly do not play in any of the Shakespearian adaptations, for example. Rather, the resemblances show that Tate resorted to proven theatrical traditions when writing his play and returned to these, as well as his previous play, in writing the libretto for *Dido*.

Tate's libretto and play are also related, and different from Virgil, in that Dido never appears in a happy state. First she is tormented by her illicit passion, then by her fall from chastity as a result of a single indiscretion. Unlike Virgil's Dido, Tate's heroine never enjoys her relationship with Aeneas. Act III of the play ends with the Queen and Brutus taking refuge from the storm in a cave, as in the *Aeneid*. Act IV begins with the Queen's self-reproaches. She tells her confidante Amarante (Belinda):

> From Honor's heights which I with toil had climb'd
> How I am in a moment faln
> And plung'd in Infamy!
> Th'Almighty Pow'rs beheld; and yet created
> No Prodigy to awe me from the Danger.
> My stupid Vertue slept,
> My Guardian Genius slept,
> The planets idlely gaz'd,
> And all the Starry Host
> Sat unconcern'd Spectators of my Fate!

[27] Price, *Henry Purcell*, 231–2. See also Robert Craven, 'Nahum Tates's Third *Dido and Aeneas*: The Sources of the Libretto to Purcell's Opera', *The World of Opera*, 1 (1979), 65–78, for a discussion of Shadwell's play and Tate's *Brutus of Alba* in relation to Tate's libretto.

My struggling on the Rock
But Tortures me the more;
I'm stabbed with thousand Deaths, but cannot die!

She vows to avenge herself by killing Brutus and sending him
screaming to 'th'Abyss of Fire' (sounding much like Virgil's
Dido), but when he enters, she finds herself powerless to do the
deed and orders him to leave instead. Brutus counters with,

Hold, hold! by all that's good
Let me conjure you stifle that rash voice!

and begs for her continued favours.

This scene is the antecedent for the confrontation between
Dido and Aeneas in the libretto. Dido enters with her confidante.
She complains that 'earth and heaven conspire[d] her fall', and it
must be understood that this occurred not through heavenly
intervention, as in Virgil, but because all nature truly sat by
'idlely' and 'unconcern'd' as in *Brutus*. When she accuses Aeneas
of hypocrisy, he starts to answer, as does Brutus, 'By all that's
good . . .', but Dido cuts him off. Ultimately he leaves unhappily
and unwillingly.

In both versions Dido also dies without doing physical violence
to herself. She is destroyed from within. In the play the Queen
speaks clearly to her confidante:

My malady at last has prov'd my Cure,
My Griefs at last have swell'd to that degree,
To break my o're-charg'd Heart and give me Ease.
Death thou hast shun'd me long, long fail'd my hopes,
But now I've seized thee, and I'll hold thee fast.   [dies

(Act V)

As in Tate's use of witches, the dramatic situation of a woman
succumbing to death following an illicit sexual encounter had
important antecedents in earlier seventeenth-century drama,
where, in fact, death had been the traditional response to seduction or rape.[28] The abused women sometimes took their own
lives, as in the story of Lucretia, but in at least two previous plays

[28] Suzanne Gossett, '"Best men are molded out of faults"; Marrying the rapist in
Jacobean Drama', *English Literary Renaissance*, xiv (1984), 305–27.

the fall from chastity is described as sufficiently fatal in itself. In these cases, the victim suffers an immediate physical change that reveals her fallen state and points to her imminent death. In *Valentinian* (1612) by John Fletcher, Lucina is raped by Valentinian. When her husband finds her weeping he knows immediately what has occurred. He says,

> Already in thy teares, I have read thy wrongs,
> . . . ;   go thou Lilly,
> Thou sweetly dropping floure: go silver Swan,
> And sing thine owne sad requiem . . .

Her handmaiden later reports that when her mistress entered 'the house weeping and blushing, "Dare I, said she, defile this house with whore, / In which his noble family has flourish'd? / At which she fel, and stird no more"' (III.i. 366–8).[29] Apparently, Lucina, like the Queen in Tate's play, simply expires from a broken 'o're-charg'd Heart'. Only five years before *Dido and Aeneas*, *Valentinian* was revised and performed in London with music by Louis Grabu.

In Philip Massinger's *The Unnatural Combat* (1624–5), this outcome is even more clearly depicted. Theocrine is raped. Afterwards her condition is obvious and 'her father hardly recognizes her. "Who is this? how alter'd! how deform'd!" She tells him, "I am dead indeed to all but misery / O come not neere me sir, I am infectious. . ."'(V.ii. 186–8,190,197–8).[30] Her death follows without additional cause, as she explains in her last words:

> [Montrevile] Abus'd me sir by violence, and this told
> I cannot live to speake more; may the cause
> In you finde pardon, but the speeding curse
> Of a ravish'd maid fall heavie, heavie on him.
> *Beaufort* my lawfull love, farewell for ever.   [She dies]
>   (V.ii.212–16)[31]

The similarity of situation in Massinger's play and *Brutus of Alba* should be obvious. Tate's use of this convention, moreover, implies much about the relationship of the leading characters not only in his play, but also in the opera, which is so closely modelled

---

[29] Ibid., 308.   [30] Ibid., 326.   [31] Ibid.

on it. The libretto translates Dido's final words into a more ambiguous statement:

> Thy hand, Belinda, darkness shades me,
> On thy bosom let me rest,
> More I would but death invades me.
> Death is now a welcome Guest.

However, the meaning should by now be clear. Dido, seduced by Aeneas, loses her chastity and therefore her life. It is impossible, in light of the literary tradition and the close relation of *Brutus of Alba* to Tate's later libretto, to assume, as Price does, that Tate intended Dido to remain alive at the end of the opera. Even though 'none of the main sources of the opera . . . includes a stage direction for her death',[32] the stage direction '*Cupids* appear in the Clouds o're her Tomb' appears along with the line in the final chorus: 'To scatter Roses on her Tomb', and Dido repeatedly speaks of death.

In this scene, as in many others, the close relationship between Tate's play and libretto helps to explain the actions of the main characters in the latter, where the plot has been so distilled to be at times difficult to understand. The motivation of the Sorceress, the final confrontation of Dido and Aeneas, and Dido's death can only be fully understood by comparison with the play. The parallel structure of these two dramas also helps to clarify the stage action, as can be seen particularly in the two hunting scenes.

In the opera Belinda and the chorus give thanks for the beauty of the countryside, after which the Second Woman sings a song. All of this seems particularly static and unnecessary, but the play explains the action. The characters enter 'as from the Chase'. Custom decrees that 'when the sports are done / The Court repairs to the Diana Fountain, / To worship there the Goddess of the Woods / And drink of the cool Stream; / The Queen drinks first' (*Brutus*, Act III). In the play the sorceress Ragusa has poisoned the couple's bowls with a potion that 'fires the chastest breasts with loose Desires'. 'All kneel before the fountain', and Brutus and the Queen partake of the love potion. Afterwards there is 'a dance of Masquers, during which a dark Storm gathers'. As the storm breaks, Brutus and the Queen head together for

---

[32] Price, *Henry Purcell*, 261.

shelter. The witches cackle with delight. In the opera, the solo/ chorus 'Thanks to these lonesome vales' represents the worship of Diana; the song 'Oft she visits' with a dance by Dido's Women to entertain Aeneas replaces the masque.

In this scene the one difference between the play and the libretto is that the storm which ends the scene serves in the play, as in Virgil's epic, to unite the lovers; in the opera, it serves to separate them. Despite the close parallels between the play and libretto, then, the play maintains a stronger link to the *Aeneid*, and the storm is but one example. The witches of *Brutus* are also closer to their mythological predecessors by assisting in the union of Aeneas and Dido through the use of a love potion. In the opera, Dido is solely responsible for her fall. There are also specific scenes in *Brutus*, lacking in the opera, that appear to derive from Virgil.

For example, in *Brutus of Alba* the Queen's confidante calls upon the sorceress Ragusa to help the Queen 'redress her grief'. The Queen herself bows to the sorceress:

> O Prophetess powerfull in Mystick Rites,
> Be kind, and with thy sacred Art assist
> A suppliant Queen, and thou shalt be my goddess.

The idea for bringing these characters together comes apparently from the *Aeneid* where Dido dupes her sister into believing an Ethiopian priestess has taught her how to banish Aeneas from her heart (IV, 483–93).

> I have been in touch with a priestess from there, a Massylian
>   who once,
> As warden of Hesperides' sacred close, was used to
> Feed the dragon which guarded their orchard of golden apples,
> Sprinkling its food with moist honey and sedative poppy-seeds.
> Now this enchantress claims that her spells can liberate
> One's heart, or can inject love-pangs, just as she wishes;
> Can stop the flow of rivers, send the stars flying backwards,
> Conjure ghosts in the night: she can make the earth cry out
> Under one's feet, and elm trees come trooping down from the
>   mountains.
> Dear sister, I solemnly call to witness the gods and you whom
> I love, that I do not willingly resort to her magic arts.

The Dido of the opera does not resort to witchcraft or enchant-resses.

Tate's two Dido dramas also differ in that the play is closely modelled on John Dryden's *All for Love*, a play that had appeared less than a year before Tate's *Brutus*, and was based on Shakespeare's *Antony and Cleopatra*.[33] There are, of course similarities between these two stories. In both, a native queen falls in love with a foreign military officer; in both he returns her love and thereby gives up the pursuit of his glory or destiny. Tate uses Dryden's play in *Brutus of Alba* both by copying the use of blank verse and by borrowing specific details of the plot as well. Perhaps Tate was even influenced in his choice of story as Dryden himself had related the tale of Antony and Cleopatra to that of Dido and Aeneas in his prologue:

> The poet fights this day unarmed, without his rhyme;
> And bringing a tale which often has been told,
> As sad as Dido's, and almost as old.

Tate used Dryden's play to find an impetus that would impel Aeneas to forsake his Queen. In *All for Love* Antony's best friend, Ventidius, tries to galvanize the hero back to arms and away from the charms of Cleopatra by killing himself rather than Antony, as the young warrior has requested.

> ANTONY. Strike home, be sure.
> VENTIDIUS. Home as my sword will reach.   [*Kills self*
> (*All for Love*: Act V)

In *Brutus of Alba* this becomes,

> BRUTUS. Here, strike the Breast thou hast so long deceiv'd.
> ASARACUS. Yes Prince I'll strike—your Heart—that Heart of yours
> That's in my Bosome lodg'd.   [*stabs self*
> (*Brutus of Alba*: Act IV)

In *Brutus*, unlike *All for Love*, the unexpected death of the close friend succeeds in having the hero act on his friend's previous advice. Brutus vows he will mend his errant ways:

---

[33] This correlation of Dryden and Tate's plays is noted by Christopher Spencer, *Nahum Tate* (New York: Twayne Publishers, 1972), 55–63.

Give notice to the Fleet we sail to Night.
Said I to Night! forsake the Queen to Night!
Forsake! Oh Fate! the Queen! to Night forsake her!
My word is past, 'tis giv'n, and those pale Lips
With silent Oratory plead my Promise.

(Act IV)

In *Dido and Aeneas* all this is changed. Aeneas's friend is
eliminated, as are all the male characters except Aeneas and the
male chorus, perhaps for the lack of male performers at the girls'
school, but as much because Aeneas is no longer the 'pious
Aeneas' of Virgil, and so honourable a motivation no longer suits
his character. This hero, having promised to forsake his destiny,
breaks his word because he is deceived by a false Mercury. A small
echo remains, however, from Tate's previous play.

SPIRIT. Jove summons thee this night away.
AENEAS.   Tonight?
SPIRIT. Tonight thou must forsake this land.

.   .   .   .

AENEAS. Jove's commands shall be obey'd
  Tonight our anchors shall be weigh'd.

But neither a true god nor a true friend provides the Aeneas of the
opera with his motivation; he is guided by a sham.
  Brutus of Alba serves as the link between *Dido* and Dryden's *All
for Love*, just as it does between *Dido* and Virgil's epic, but a few
reminiscences of both Dryden and Virgil appear in the opera
without passing through the play. For example, after Mercury
appears to Virgil's Aeneas, the hero stands 'dumbfounded' with
his 'voice stuck in his throat'.

But oh, what was he to do? What words could he find to get
  round
The temperamental queen? How broach the matter to her?

(IV, 283–4)

In the same situation, Tate's Aeneas says,

But ah, what language can I try
My injur'd queen to pacify?

In *All for Love,* Anthony's wife and friend urge him to renounce Cleopatra, but he cries out,

> 'Tis too much,
> Too much, Octavia, I am pressed with sorrows
> Too heavy to be borne.
>
> (Act IV)

Dido, trying to repress her own feelings, echoes this sentiment.

> Ah, Belinda, I am prest
> With torment not to be confest.

Such similarities in wording, even in different situations, show that Tate did not just work from his own previous play, but went back to its two sources, just as he drew also from a number of seventeenth-century dramatic and theatrical traditions. Despite their differences, however, Tate's two Dido dramas maintain important similarities: the use of stock English witches not mythological gods, the single night shared by Dido and Aeneas, the motivation for Aeneas's departure coming from within the confines of the play, and the non-violent death of Dido. In fact, the close relation of Tate's two dramas can be easily confirmed by a brief comparison of the opera and play with one potential English model and a handful of contemporary European operatic versions.

The one previous English drama based on the Dido story was written by Christopher Marlowe in the 1580s, about a hundred years before Tate's two dramas. It essentially follows the story in the *Aeneid,* although King Iarbas takes on a speaking role, and the scenes showing the substitution of Cupid for Ascanius are greatly expanded. The full panoply of mythological characters is used, and the gods, as in the *Aeneid,* motivate Aeneas's departure. In these relationships to Virgil's epic, Marlowe's play more resembles the seventeenth-century Italian operas based on this story than either of Tate's later versions. There are three: *La Didone* by Busenello, set by Cavalli (Venice, 1641), *La Didone* by Moscardini, set by Mattioli (Bologna, 1656), and *La Didone delirante* by Franceschi, set by Pallavicino (Venice, 1686). A French version following a little after Purcell's *Dido and Aeneas* also fits in this group: *Didon* by Xaintonge, set by Desmarets (Paris, 1693).[34]

These five dramas, including Marlowe's play, resemble each other in the same ways they differ from both of Tate's versions. Only one (Moscardini, 1656) avoids making an important sub-plot out of the advances of Iarbas. In Marlowe's play this character attains heroic stature when he stabs himself after Dido throws herself on the funeral pyre. Anna, who has loved him, then kills herself for his, not Dido's sake, as she does (under the name Amarante) in Tate's play. In the librettos by Busenello (1641) and Franceschi (1686) this tragic ending is avoided by having Dido marry Iarbas. And in the Paris version, Iarbas is raised to Aeneas's level in that he is also the son of an important mythological figure, Jupiter, thus allowing for the interpolation of additional mythological scenes calling for elaborate scenic effects, dancing, and choral singing. Finally, when Dido dies, as she does in three of these five dramas, it is violently—either by sword, fire, or both. Having her marry Iarbas, as she does in the other two, is a concession to the convention of the *lieto fine*, or happy ending, of Baroque music drama; it is, however, dramati-cally unsupportable. And it is interesting that the man who could write a happy ending for *King Lear* avoided the superimposition of such an ending in both of his Dido dramas. The similarity of *Dido and Aeneas* to *Brutus of Alba* and the relationship of these dramas to seventeenth-century English dramatic conventions and to Dryden in particular set them apart from English Renaissance drama as well as from foreign operatic models. The stuttering servants of Moscardini's version (1656) along with its passionate love scene between Dido and Aeneas, and the transvestite dis-guises of Franceschi's version (1686), underscore how different these traditions could be.

The strong ties between *Dido* and *Brutus* and other English seventeenth-century dramas illustrate that the individual charac-ters and actions of the opera are unlikely to have specific, contemporary, allegorical meanings. In order to argue that *Dido* is

[34] The Italian librettos are preserved in the Schatz libretto collection at The Library of Congress, Washington, DC: their numbers are 1718 (Busenello), 6102 (Moscardini), and 7736 (Franceschi). The French libretto may be found in *Recueil Général des Opéra représentéz par l'Academie Royale de Musique depuis son Établissement*, IV (Paris, 1703), 281–344. I am very grateful to Howard M. Brown for making these sources available to me.

a political allegory, therefore, one must either create far-fetched relations between *Dido* and *Brutus* or negate this relation altogether. For example, Buttrey accepts the strong relationship between Tate's play and libretto, and defends the allegory in the latter by trying to show that the play, too, was politically allegorical. He argues that the Queen of Syracuse (Dido) represents Charles II and that the scheming lords plotting her downfall represent specific figures in Charles's court. He fails, however, to explain what person or persons could possibly have been represented by Aeneas or the witches, or why the Queen simply expires at the end. Price, on the other hand, deliberately underestimates the importance of literary precedents in *Dido*,[35] stating simply that 'the influence of *Brutus of Alba* on *Dido and Aeneas* has been exaggerated'.[36] However, the close parallels between Tate's two dramas in their plots, scenic layout, and even their texts cannot be so easily dismissed.

In order to prove a contemporary allegorical reading it would be necessary to show that Tate's use of witches, of a single night of indiscretion, of an ironic worship of Diana, goddess of chastity, either immediately before or after Dido loses this virtue, and of Dido's death as a direct result of her fallen state are unrelated in his two dramas, for no one can argue that *Brutus* allegorizes William and Mary eleven years before their accession. Furthermore, in order to give allegorical readings or Purcell's music as a reason for the relative obscurity of *Dido*, it would be necessary to explain why no other work of this type, (for example, John Blow's *Venus and Adonis* [*c.*1685]), was transferred to the public stage, why 'Ah, Belinda' could appear in print in 1698 in *Orpheus Britannicus* (see Plate 8) while William was still living, or why the opera could have been publicly performed in 1700 during William's lifetime. Finally, in order to assign to Purcell the blame for his opera's lack of performances, one must show that the musical depiction of Dido's death is indeed a misinterpretation of the text, which in light of the parallels between *Brutus* and *Dido* seems highly unlikely.

The function of *Dido* as a morality rather than a political allegory is buttressed, strangely enough, by the 1700 public performance of the opera in the Gildon version of Shakespeare's

---

[35] Price, *Henry Purcell*, 231, n. 11.   [36] Ibid., 226.

Measure for Measure.[37] In this play Claudio is condemned to die for having sexual relations with his betrothed Julietta, because Angelo, the deputy for the absent Duke, has enforced an old law against fornication. As Price writes, the performance of the opera is arranged 'to show Angelo the possible consequences of enforcing too zealously a law against nature'.[38] As Price continues, 'The allegory implies an interpretation of the central ambiguity of *Dido and Aeneas* in direct opposition to almost all modern criticism: in the new context, the lovers have committed a sin punished by the havoc wrought when the Sorceress tricks Aeneas into abandoning the queen.'[39] Surely, it is more important that the opera was used in this way only eleven years after its composition than that 'modern criticism' has failed to see the story as a morality showing the gentlewomen of Chelsea the results of sinful behaviour.

The argument against a political reading is further strengthened when Angelo, as Price has shown, deliberately misreads the moral allegory and sees himself in the role of Aeneas, as an adventuring and false seducer who has the same 'love 'em and leave 'em' philosophy as the sailors. That is, Aeneas's rather debased character in the libretto is only emphasized in *Measure for Measure* where the hypocritical ruler lusts after the innocent Isabella. After seeing the scene showing the witches plotting Dido's fall, Angelo, who is holding Isabella's brother prisoner, comments to himself:

> This scene just hits my case; her brother's danger
> Is here the storm must furnish blest occasion;
> And when, my Dido, I've possess'd thy charms,
> I then will throw thee from my glutted arms,
> And think no more on all thy soothing harms.

If there was any thought that Aeneas allegorically represented William, a public performance in which the role of Aeneas was likened to that of the morally corrupt Angelo, who is standing in for the rightful ruler much as the Dutch William could be thought to be standing in for a rightful English king, would have been totally impossible.

[37] The textbook for Gildon's adaptation of *Measure for Measure* complete with the text of *Dido and Aeneas* is preserved at the British Library, London.
[38] Ibid., 236.
[39] Ibid., 236–7.

Dido and Aeneas was written for a private occasion, as its most important all-sung predecessors had been, and like its predecessors it was not performed on the public stage where plays with musical interludes and spectacle were preferred. Its libretto was derived by the librettist from an earlier play of his own that had already altered the Virgil legend—in part following a dramatic tradition that dealt with rape and seduction. The Epilogue by Thomas D'Urfey, which was spoken by Lady Dorothy Burke and refers to the contemporary political situation, has sometimes been used to support a political reading of the Dido story, but the main subject of this poem offers yet one more corroboration of the view that the Dido legend was suitably adapted as a morality for the girls of Josias Priest's boarding school who acted the drama.

> All that we know the angels do above,
> I've read, is that they sing and that they love,
> The vocal part we have tonight perform'd
> And if by Love our hearts not yet are warm'd
> Great Providence has still more bounteous been
> To save us from those grand deceivers, men.

3

Text: Literary Style

The two factors most responsible for the independence of *Dido* from Tate's previous play are, first, the maturity of its author, and second, its function as a libretto. *Brutus of Alba*, after all, was Tate's first play. In the eleven years between it and the opera, Tate had produced his three famous (now infamous) Shakespearian adaptations, *The History of King Richard the Second* (1680), *The History of King Lear* (1681), and *The Ingratitude of a Commonwealth or, The Fall of Caius Martius Coriolanus* (1682). Other adaptations also appeared during this interim: *A Duke and no Duke* (from Aston Cokain, 1685), *Cuckolds-Haven: or, an Alderman No Conjurer* (from Jonson, 1685), and *The Island Princess* (from Fletcher, 1689). And Tate had also added another original tragedy to his list of works, *The Loyal General* (1680). Meanwhile he had composed much poetry and published a number of translations, and only three years after the production of *Dido*, he was appointed poet laureate. Thus the writing of this libretto gave Tate the opportunity as a mature author to go back to the subject that had formed his first drama. But Tate was no longer writing a play; that he concerned himself with the necessities of an operatic libretto affected the result as much or more than his growth in experience.

Because it takes substantially longer to sing a text than to speak it, a libretto cannot be as expansive as a play, neither in overall length, nor, generally speaking, in the number of lines given to a single character at any one time. This is even more true for *Dido*, which was apparently intended to be a short production—the three main acts take little more than an hour to perform and thus hardly constitute a full evening's entertainment. Tate used this restriction to tighten his original drama; in the printed libretto the entire text of *Dido and Aeneas* covers only five and a half pages. All of the characters not strictly necessary to the story are omitted from the libretto—the vengeful Lord of the Queen's court, the aggressive ambassadors from the Agrigentine court, and Aeneas's friend and his son are all deleted. Although it is noteworthy, in light of the performance by and for the residents of a girls' boarding school, that all are male, these omissions at once improve the thrust of the plot by making it less diffuse and add to a heightened sense of intimacy. *Dido and Aeneas* is a chamber piece as much in content as in size.

A reduction also occurs in individual speeches. The longest, of ten lines, allows Aeneas a chance to respond to the effects of the Spirit's command. Other potentially lengthy speeches are carefully broken up—as in Act II where the Sorceress's plotting of sixteen lines is so interrupted by laughter and eager questioning that the longest remaining segment is of six lines. In the play, on the other hand, seven line speeches are the norm, and those with more than twenty lines occur with regularity; the longest consists of twenty-eight lines.

Another important difference between the play and libretto involves the use of rhyme in the latter. Seventeenth-century English writers clearly felt that sung text should be rhymed, perhaps because rhyme was considered inherently musical. In this Dryden was certainly an influence.

Tate had copied Dryden's use of blank verse in *All for Love* (1677) for his *Brutus of Alba* written the next year. This was also the period during which Dryden began toying with opera; his first, *The State of Innocence* (1677), based on Milton's *Paradise Lost*, was never performed. His next, however, *Albion and Albanius* (1685), had a modest success, set, albeit poorly, by the French composer Louis Grabu. Dryden in his Preface takes pains to explain their endeavour. He states outright that 'an *Opera* is a poetical tale' but warns that 'lofty, figurative, and majestical' expressions are out of place in a text to be sung. Indeed he allows that one should strive 'to please the Hearing, rather than to gratify the understanding'. Thus 'Rhyme' must 'take [the] place of Reason'. Dryden also strongly implies that the lines must be short and consonants avoided, and he admits this to be a difficult task indeed.

> The same reasons which depress thought in an Opera, have a Stronger effect upon the Words; especially in our Language: for there is no maintaining the purity of English in short measures, where the Rhyme returns so quick, and is so often Female, or

double Rhyme, which is not natural to our Tongue, because it consists too much of Monosyllables, and those too, most commonly clogg'd with Consonants . . .[40]

Such linguistic considerations had played a large role in the minds of English writers throughout the century. Dryden's remarks were anticipated, for example, somewhat more than thirty years previously by Richard Flecknoe in his Preface to *Ariadne* (1654), a work he intended to be set to music.

Now the advantage the Italian tongue hath of ours in it, is chiefly, as I conceive, in the strength of their words, they being composed more of the A, and O (the sinewousness of a Tongue) as also the length of them, whereby each one is able to sustain it self, whereas our Language is so debile and weak, as our words die in a manner as soon as born, not being able scarcely to brook the air; Ending also so faintly and feebly for want of length, as they are forced to fall upon the next following for their support, whence comes the difficulty of pronouncing our words distinctly, or understanding our Language when it is sung, which inconvenience to Remedy, I concluded first, That your long discourses, and periods, were carefully to be avoided by us, in Recitative Musick, that so the often coming to a close, might make up in the full stop, our words want of length, and by severall reprises more strengthen them.[41]

Although rhyme, repetition, and short verses were thus accepted early on as integral parts of an English libretto, rhyme schemes continued to be debated. The rhymed couplet always garnered the most support, but as early as 1650 William Davenant (in the Preface to his heroic poem *Gondibert*) had suggested a rhymed quatrain (ABAB) as better suited to music by having more breadth than repeated couplets.[42] General consensus finally decided that no one pattern should hold throughout. Thus Samuel Pepys wrote in his diary (13 February 1666) that the composer Captain Cooke 'was fain to direct Sir William Davenant in the breaking of his verses into such and such lengths'.[43]

[40] Dryden, Preface to *Albion and Albanius* (1685) in *Essays*, i. 278.

[41] As quoted in Eugene Haun, *But Hark! More Harmony: Libretti of Restoration Opera in English* (Ypsilanti, Mich.: Eastern Michigan University Press, 1971), 37–8.

[42] Sir William Davenant, Preface to *Gondibert*, ed. David F. Gladish (Oxford: Oxford University Press, 1971), 17.

[43] Samuel Pepys, *The Diary of Samuel Pepys*, ed. Robert Latham and William Matthews (Berkeley: University of California Press, 1974), viii, 59.

By the time of *Dido and Aeneas* in 1689, therefore, a common body of thought in seventeenth-century England called for librettos that rhymed, had short discourses, short verses of mixed lengths, frequent stops, frequent repetitions, double rhymes where possible, and words that emphasized vowel rather than consonant sounds. Dryden assimilated all these rules in *Albion and Albanius* where he tried to practise them. Tate follows the suggestions faithfully.

There is, for example, the opening lyric of Act I.

> Shake the Cloud from off your Brow.
> Fate your wishes does allow.
> > Empire Growing,
> > Pleasures Flowing,
> Fortune smiles and so should you.
> Shake the Cloud from off your Brow.

All the rules obtain—the short stanza, the use of rhyme (sometimes double), the short verses of different lengths, the frequent stops, and the use of a refrain—but particularly remarkable are the numbers of open vowel sounds with as few 'clogg'd consonants' as the language permits.

This lyric can be compared, first, to the parallel passage from *Brutus of Alba*, which will illustrate how and to what extent spoken speech could differ from sung speech in seventeenth-century English stage works.

> Content smiles on each *Syracusian*'s Brow,
> Who for the safety of our Widdow'd Realm
> Wait your Espousels with your Royal Guest,
> To wed your Persons and your States Together;
> For this the suppliant Crowd to th'Altars throng,
> Where with religious violence and joint prayers
> They storm and press the Heavens into Compliance.
>
> (Act I)

There is no rhyme, no emphasis on open vowel sounds; the lines are long, as is the sentence structure, and there are many 'clogg'd consonants', as in, for example, 'widdow'd realm' or 'suppliant crowd'.

The opening lyrics of *Dido* can also be compared to a similarly structured sung text from Dryden's *Albion*.

> O Hermes! pity mee!
> I was, while Heav'n did smile
> The Queen of all this Isle,
>   Europe's Pride
>   And Albion's Bride;
> But gone my Plighted Lord! ah, gone is Hee!
> O Hermes! pity mee!

Despite the similar structure, however, Dryden's lyrics differ from Tate's by emphasizing the *i* and *e* vowels, which are harder to sing, and they contain the 'clogg'd consonants' Tate's lyric lacks, at, for example, 'Europe's pride' or 'plighted Lord'. Tate's talent for writing verse that is easily singable has never been sufficiently praised; his ability to change blank verse into text suitable for musical setting is particularly remarkable. In this regard, even if in this regard only, he stands above all his seventeenth-century compatriots.

Tate's typical verse pattern for declamation consists of rhyming couplets with four and sometimes five stresses.

> DIDO. Whence could so much virtue spring?
>   What storms, what battles did he sing!
>   Anchises valour mix'd with Venus' charms,
>   How soft in peace and yet how fierce in arms.
> BELINDA. A tale so strong and full of woe
>   Might melt the rocks as well as you.
> SECOND WOMAN. What stubborn heart unmov'd could see
>   Such distress, such piety.

Sometimes this pattern is broken to end a scene. For example, Dido concludes the dialogue above with this set of verses.

> DIDO. Mine with storms of care oppress'd
>   Is taught to pity the distress'd.
>   Mean wretches fate can touch—
>   So soft, so sensible my breast—
>   But ah! I fear I pity him too much.

The rhyme scheme of AABAB gives greater breadth than couplets could to this concluding speech.

Tate was not a prisoner to conventional schemes, and moments of great emotion in the text particularly call forth altered verse forms. For example, the tension of the moment when the Spirit commands Aeneas to leave Dido contains lines of varying length in a rhyme scheme unique within the libretto: (the number of stresses in each line are given in parentheses) A (4), B (4), A (4), B (5), C (4), D (4), D (4), C (3), C (3). The longest line represents Aeneas's dalliance in Carthage: 'The angry god will brook no longer stay', after which the increasing shortness of line adds to the urgency of the commanded departure.

> SPIRIT. Stay, Prince, and hear great Jove's command,
> He summons thee this night away.
> Tonight thou must forsake this land,
> The angry god will brook no longer stay,
> Jove commands thee waste no more,
> In love's delights those precious hours,
> Allowed by th'almighty powers,
> To gain th'Hesperian shore,
> And ruined Troy restore.

The most unusual verse scheme occurs in Dido's final air, to be sung as she is dying. Its remarkable flexibility perhaps depicts the loosening of life's hold.

> DIDO. When I am laid in earth, may my wrongs create
> No trouble in thy breast!
> Remember me—but ah! forget my fate.

This represents the most notable feature of Tate's literary talent— his ability to write texts that are inherently suited to musical setting, but that are flexible enough not only to allow variety but also to reflect the sense of the words they contain.

Tate's care with the style of his versification throughout the opera carries over into other aspects of his libretto. For example, he takes specific images and weaves them into the fabric of the libretto as one means of tightening the construction. The most pervasive of these refers to fate.

In the opening song Belinda sings to Dido, 'fate your wishes does allow'. Later in this scene the chorus becomes more aggressive: 'When monarchs unite . . . they *triumph* . . . o'er . . . their fate'. When Dido tells Aeneas, 'Fate forbids what you pursue,' Aeneas answers, 'Aeneas has no fate but you' and offers to 'defy' any other. Thus in these opening scenes a gradual progression takes place in the human reference to fate—from fate allowing, to triumphing over fate, to defiance of fate.

In the second act the humans take a more submissive attitude. The Second Woman sings of how 'Actaeon met his fate', and almost immediately Aeneas meets his and worries about Dido's—'How can so hard a fate be took?' In the last air of the opera Dido meets hers—'Remember me, but ah! forget my fate'.

Another theme seems to relate the metaphorical flames of passion with actual fire. Thus, in Act I Aeneas sings, 'Ah! make not, in a hopeless fire, a hero fall, and Troy once more expire,' comparing his inward passion to the burning of Troy. Belinda refers to Dido's passion as a flame immediately afterwards, saying that the Queen's 'eyes confess the flame her tongue denies', and at the beginning of Act II, the Sorceress transfers this image to Dido's city when she sings of 'a mischief shall make all Carthage flame'. The final reference occurs in Act III when the witches succeed in turning around Aeneas's first allusion to flame: 'Elissa bleeds tonight and Carthage flames tomorrow'. That is, it will not be Aeneas who burns and Troy that expires, but Dido who expires and Carthage that burns.

Other images like these stand out, although on a smaller scale. When the witches move to prepare the 'charm', the listener is perhaps meant to remember that Dido in Act I spoke of succumbing to Aeneas's 'valour' and 'charm'. The crux of the opera hangs on understanding whose 'charm'—Aeneas's or the Sorceress's—actually destroys Dido. Tate would certainly have the schoolgirls believe the former.

In Act I the courtiers, urging a union between Dido and Aeneas, sing of 'the dart that's dreadful to a warrior's heart' and Dido's power to 'heal the smart'. When the lovers part in Act III the same courtiers now sing of the couple's decision 'to shun the cure they most desire'. If, the night before, they had been able to 'shun the cure' for the 'dreadful smart', the tragic ending would not have befallen them.

Finally and most poignantly, when the courtiers sing the mourning chorus for Dido, they ask Cupids 'to scatter roses on her tomb'. In the first scene they pleaded Aeneas's case by saying, 'Cupids [will] strew your path with flowers'. The final chorus thus becomes a grim fulfilment of that earlier, happier promise.

It is clear from studying the libretto of *Dido and Aeneas* that Tate was concerned to make it as unified as possible. The use of recurrent images illustrates one side of this concern; the other is reflected in his use of the Aristotelian unities of time, place, and action. As in so many of the other aspects of the libretto, the use of the unities derives from Dryden, who in the Preface to *All for Love* states that he adheres to them in that drama 'more than is necessary on the English stage'. Tate does not follow Dryden's lead in *Brutus of Alba*, where the action is diffused by the additional characters and their individual goals, and the time period lasts three days: the day of wooing (Acts I and II), the day of winning (Act III), and the day of wailing (Acts IV and V). On the other hand, in *Dido and Aeneas* Tate follows the unities even more strictly than had Dryden.

The scenes all occur in Carthage, giving it unity of place. There is also only one action, the loss of Dido's love, and, thus, her life. Tate even adheres to the unity of time.

Although there are no specific times given in the sparse stage directions, the text itself gives enough information so that the passage of time can be discerned. Aeneas's lament after hearing the edict of the false Mercury gives the clue to the temporal layout of the entire opera.

> No sooner she resigns her heart
> But from her arms I'm forced to part;
> How can so hard a fate be took?
> One night enjoy'd, the next forsook.

That is, Act I must occur at some time in one day, and Acts II and III occur in the morning and evening of the next. The time span of the last two acts is further clarified in other dialogue. In Act II, for example, the Sorceress speaks of ruining the Queen by nightfall ('The Queen of Carthage ... ere sunset shall most wretched prove'). During this scene the hunt, happening simultaneously, is heard, and thus when the Spirit speaks to Aeneas later he charges him leave 'tonight'. In the third act evening approaches, and the witches sing of 'Phoebe's pale deluding beams / Gliding o'er deceitful streams!' Thus the second act must occur in the morning, as would be a likely time for a hunt, and the third act occurs later that afternoon. The opera ends just at sunset. The only difficulty, then, comes in the placement of the first act, for it contains no textual clues. But if it occurs at night (like Act II of *Brutus*), say at an evening banquet in Aeneas's honour (such as happens in Virgil's *Aeneid*) then unity of time has been achieved, the action occurring within one revolution of the sun. Since Dido and Aeneas do go off together at the end of Act I, this solution seems likely.

In the observation of the unities, in the adaptation of an epic episode into an entity, in the alteration of the text to make it suitable for musical setting, and in the transformation of Dido into a tragic heroine, *Dido and Aeneas* is far removed from its classical origin in Virgil's *Aeneid*. It, of course, has become a true Restoration product, tied to previous dramatic conventions and the burgeoning English operatic tradition. It was also tailored to suit its inaugural performance at the Chelsea boarding school of Mr Josias Priest, thereby becoming a morality play. But this does not mean it has lost all relation to classical literature, for its alterations from Virgil and its adaptations to English traditions have transformed it into an Aristotelian tragedy.[44] It is an action, complete in itself, that adheres to the unities of time, place, and action; it contains a tragic heroine whose misfortunes are brought upon her by an error of judgement; its language has rhythm and harmony with song added to it; and it is in dramatic, not narrative, form, with incidents arousing pity and, at least in the case of the Chelsea schoolgirls, fear. The libretto of *Dido and Aeneas* is an extraordinary work of art that holds the power to redeem its author from accusations of mediocrity and infamy.

[44] Aristotle writes in his *Poetics*, 'A tragedy, then, is the imitation of an action that is serious and also, as having magnitude, complete in itself; in language with pleasurable accessories, each kind brought in separately in the parts of the work; in a dramatic, not in a narrative form; with incidents arousing pity and fear, where with to accomplish its catharsis of such emotions. Here by "language with pleasurable accessories" I mean that with rhythm and harmony or song superadded; and by "the kinds separately" I mean that some portions are worked out with verse only, and others in turn with song' (as quoted in *Introduction to Aristotle*, ed. Richard McKeon [New York: Random House, 1947], 631).

Part II
The Music

Introduction to Part II

The sources of *Dido and Aeneas* fall into two categories: textual and musical. The textual sources comprise the libretto from 1689 and textbooks from performances in 1700, 1774, and 1787. None of the musical sources, which include six complete manuscript scores and various sets of parts, pre-date the second half of the eighteenth century. All the sources, both textual and musical, may be compared on the basis of their texts.

The earliest surviving source is the libretto for the first performance in 1689; the dating of this libretto has been discussed above. In 1700 Purcell's opera was used by Charles Gildon in an adaptation of Shakespeare's *Measure for Measure*, where the original text was altered and expanded, a dated playbook from this production survives (see Plate 5).[1] The earliest musical source, the Tenbury manuscript, probably dates from about 1775 on account of the paper on which it is written.[2] However, its antiquated style of musical notation points to a source, no longer extant, dating from the late seventeenth or early eighteenth century. Tenbury is the only musical source to preserve a notational style contemporary with the opera's composition, which, in addition to its being the earliest surviving score, greatly enhances its importance.

The text of the Tenbury manuscript, however, does not follow either of the earlier textual sources directly. Not only are there small changes throughout, but a substantial amount of material is apparently lacking: the Prologue, the final chorus and dance in Act II of the libretto, and many other dances throughout. Additionally the layout of the text is different from that found in either

---

[1] This production is closely examined by Eric Walter White, 'New Light on *Dido and Aeneas*', in *Henry Purcell (1659–1695): Essays on his Music*, ed. Imogen Holst (London: Oxford University Press, 1959), 14–34; and by Price, *Henry Purcell*, 234–8.

[2] Although James Whatman paper, on which the Tenbury manuscript is written, was manufactured as early as 1740, the specific watermark of the JW cypher attached to the Strasbourg bend under a fleur-de-lis was not used by Whatman until after 1777. The countermark of 'JWhatman' was first used in 1760. See Thomas Balston, *James Whatman, Father and Son* (London; Methuen, 1957), and Frederick Hudson, 'The Earliest Paper Made by James Whatman the Elder (1702–1759) and its Significance in Relation to G. F. Handel and John Walsh', *The Music Review*, xxxvlii (1977), 15.

previous source. If each of Tate's three acts are thought of as having two scenes—the first and last acts both dividing at the entrance of Aeneas, and the second act including the grove scene and the cave scene—then Tate's division could be schematized: I (1–2); II (3–4); III (5–6). In 1700 this was altered to: I (1–2); II (4–3); III (5–6). In the Tenbury manuscript the act and scene divisions are: I (1–2–3); II (4); III (5–6).

All later musical sources follow the Tenbury manuscript in its deletions and layout. Thus they all must have been copied from the Tenbury itself, or from its source, now lost. The most important score among these is the Tatton Park manuscript; it is dated 1784 and signed by its copyist Philip Hayes.[3] Discovered only in the 1960s, it is the closest to the Tenbury in content. Some important differences in musical detail, however, indicate that it was probably not copied from Tenbury directly, but from the same original source, thus giving it an important value independent of Tenbury.[4] Tatton Park, however, contains many of the same faults of modernization found in the other scores from the second half of the eighteenth century (as will be shown below), and thus, although it offers clarification of some musical details and is certainly more authentic than any of the later manuscripts, it cannot claim the primacy of the Tenbury score.

At about the same time as Tenbury and Tatton Park were copied, there were two performances of *Dido and Aeneas* in London by the Academy of Ancient Music as documented by the surviving textbooks of 1774 and 1787. The text for these performances again follows the idiosyncrasies of the Tenbury in layout and omissions, but with still further changes and omissions that make it possible to identify definitively the musical sources that derive from these performances. For example, the role of Belinda reverts in name to Virgil's Anna, Aeneas's monologue at the end of Act II is shortened to a single couplet, and a number of dances, including the Triumphing Dance, are omitted altogether. By using these and other changes, three complete scores and a set of parts can be identified as deriving from the late eighteenth-century Academy performances: BL Add. MS31450, perhaps copied by J. P. Hobler (1784), and BL Add. MS 15979 copied by Edward Woodley Smith (c.1790); Folger F 770 (late eighteenth

[3] See Nigel Fortune, 'A New Purcell Source', *Music Review*, xxv (1964), 109–13.

[4] This conclusion is also reached by Margaret Laurie, ed. *Dido and Aeneas*, Preface.

century); and RAM 25 A and D (sets of parts). The musical variants contained in these sources, including the transposition of the parts of Belinda, the Sorceress, and Sailor down an octave into the alto, bass, and tenor clefs respectively, will be discussed in some detail below and in Chapter 5.

The latest of the surviving manuscripts is the Ohki manuscript preserved in the Nanki Music Library of Tokyo. Since it repeats a number of changes found in the Academy sources, it can be shown to post-date those performances; Imogen Holst has dated it *c*.1810 on the basis of the handwriting.[5] It is an important manuscript in that it illustrates in many places a clear attempt to return to the more complete readings that pre-date the Academy performances, but, once again, the idiosyncrasies of the Tenbury manuscript are all preserved.

The Tenbury manuscript can thus be identified as the earliest of the surviving scores and parts; it is also the only musical source written in the notational style of the late seventeenth century. Moreover, this manuscript is representative of the later musical sources, all of which differ from the 1689 libretto in the same ways. The variants may be enumerated as follows:

1. All lack a setting of the Prologue.
2. All lack a setting for the chorus and dance at the end of the 1689 libretto's Act II.
3. All contain apparently no more than four of the dances cued by the 1689 libretto.
4. All assign many lines, especially those relating to the part of Belinda, differently than in the 1689 libretto.
5. All divide the six scenes 3 + 1 + 2 rather than 2 + 2 + 2, as in the 1689 libretto.

The consistency of the musical sources in these important aspects means that the Tenbury manuscript may be taken as the primary representative of the group. This does not mean, of course, that the Tenbury manuscript is a copy of Purcell's original score. Indeed, it is clear that this source does not directly relate either to the 1689 libretto or to the 1700 performance, where the Prologue still appears and the scenes are in a different order than

---

[5] Imogen Holst, 'A Note on the Nanki Collection of Purcell's Works', in *Henry Purcell (1659–1695): Essays on his Music*, Appendix C, 127–30. See also *Catalogue of Rare Books and Notes: the Ohki Collection, Nanki Music Library* (Tokyo, 1970).

in any of the surviving scores. Between 1700 and 1774, the date of the first Academy production, there is only one documented set of performances; these occurred in 1704 when *Dido and Aeneas* was performed as an afterpiece to two different plays.[6] No textbook survives from these productions. Nevertheless, it is logical to assume, and we shall see that there is good reason for such an assumption, that the reading of the Tenbury manuscript and, by analogy, all of the musical sources derive from the performances of 1704.

Even if it is possible to date the origin of the music preserved for *Dido and Aeneas*, however, the relation between the musical sources and Purcell's original will not have been determined. After all, the 1704 performances represent the second revision of the opera made after the death of the composer. Part II, which focuses on the music, will therefore begin with (1) a study of the discrepancies among the texts of the 1689 libretto, the playbook from the 1700 performance, and the Tenbury score (as representative of all the musical sources) with an eye towards determining the relative merit of the musical source. Then, turning to the question of omissions in the Tenbury score, it will be possible (2) to look at Purcell's use of chorus and dance within the opera and finally (3) to investigate the overall musical structure of the work. After these discussions, emphasizing the Tenbury manuscript itself, Purcell's compositional practices will be examined more closely by analysing (4) musical declamation in *Dido* and (5) the use of repetitive (ground) basses in dances and airs.

---

[6] *Dido and Aeneas* was performed as an afterpiece to *The Anatomist* by Edward Ravenscroft on 29 January 1704; on this occasion the masque of *Mars and Venus* was apparently substituted for the Prologue. On 17 February 1704 this play was repeated with '4 musical entertainments' including *Mars and Venus*; either three of the musical entertainments were once again the three acts of *Dido* or Purcell's opera was replaced. On 8 April 1704 *Dido* appeared as an endpiece to *The Man of Mode* by Sir George Etherege, apparently without *Mars and Venus*. (See *The London Stage (1660–1800)*, Part 2: 1700–29, ed. Emmett L. Avery [Carbondale, Il., 1960], vol. I, 55, 58, and 63.)

4

The Tenbury Manuscript:
Discrepancies between it and the
Printed Texts

A comparison of the texts of the 1689 libretto, the 1700 playbook, and the Tenbury manuscript shows that all possible relations apply. The two printed texts are sometimes like one another and different from the manuscript score; the later two sources are sometimes alike, and different from the 1689 libretto; the 1700 playbook is sometimes different from both the libretto and the manuscript; and all three sources are sometimes different from one another. Thus from the outset there are clearly three possible interpretations for the discrepancies: (1) that Purcell deliberately altered Tate's libretto, (2) that printing errors in the original libretto were corrected in the later versions, or (3) that alterations were made to the libretto (and score) after the first performance, either for the 1700 production or later. Undoubtedly all these statements are true in part, for no one explanation can account for all the textual variations.

In a few cases it is clear that the 1689 libretto is in error. For example, at the end of Act I, the libretto assigns the following quatrain to Dido.

> Fate forbids what you Ensue
> *Aeneas* has no Fate but you.
> Let *Dido* smile, and I'le defie,
> The feeble stroke of Destiny.

In both the 1700 playbook and the musical score, Dido is rightly given only the first line (with 'ensue' corrected to 'pursue'), and Aeneas speaks the next three. In Act III, the libretto assigns Aeneas the final line of three that all rightfully belong to Belinda.

> See Madam where the Prince appears,
> Such sorrow in his Looks he bears,
> As wou'd convince you still he's true.

As in the first instance, this error is corrected in the later versions of the text.

In these situations, the version in the libretto is obviously wrong because it is dramatically unsupportable, and, because the later versions agree upon a correction that makes dramatic sense, these versions can be accepted as authentic. In both cases one can assume that Purcell worked from an earlier, handwritten, source that did not contain these faults.

In other cases, deciding between versions is more difficult. For example, in Act II, scene i, the libretto attributes the following couplet to a single Inchanteress.

> Say *Beldam* what's thy will,
> Harms our Delight and Mischief all our skill.

In 1700, the first line is assigned to a 'witch'; the second is given to chorus. Neither version is clearly wrong dramatically. The Tenbury manuscript, however, follows the playbook and not the libretto. It would seem, then, that the version in the later sources is the correct one, for otherwise one must assume that the Tenbury manuscript is so altered from the original score that a chorus has been substituted for a solo. Since there is no reason at all for such a conclusion, it would appear that this variant in the libretto either represents another printing error, as those above, or that it offers an illustration of the possibility that Purcell deliberately altered the original libretto for musical reasons—that is, that Purcell made the decision to have a chorus at this point.

This example indicates that it is sometimes possible to use the musical setting to determine the correct textual reading from among the sources. For example, the surviving music would seem to indicate the correct dispensation of the lines:

> Thanks to these lovesome (lonesome) vailes,
> These desert hills and dales.
> So fair the game, so rich the sport,
> Diana's self might to these woods resort.

The 1689 libretto simply indicates 'Belinda' before the first couplet, and 'chorus' before the second. The 1700 playbook assigns the entire quatrain to Belinda and adds 'Repeat this cho.' in reference only to the second couplet. The Tenbury manuscript offers a slightly different solution. Each couplet has been set to a single musical line repeated in the pattern AABB'. This is sung first by Belinda in its entirety, and then the whole pattern is repeated by the chorus. Although it is possible in this case to say that the score clarifies what is merely ambiguous in the libretto, the differences may point to yet another instance of Purcell altering Tate's libretto to create a more diversified musical setting.

The situation becomes more difficult when the 1689 and 1700 sources preserve the same reading as opposed to the later musical sources, as occurs in Act III, where both textual sources give the following ten lines to the Sorceress alone (see also Plate 3).

> See the flags and streamers curling.
> Anchors weighing, sails unfurling.
> Phoebus pale deluding beames,
> Guilding o'er deceitful Streams.
> Our plot has took,
> The Queen forsook, ho, ho, ho.
> Elisas ruin'd, ho, ho, ho, next motion, [*sic*]
> Must be to storme her lover on the ocean.
> From the ruines of others our pleasures we borrow,
> Elissa bleeds tonight, and Carthage flames tomorrow.

The Tenbury manuscript divides this text into a number of segments. The first two lines are sung by the Sorceress, the next four and a half lines are given to the two witches, and the last three and a half lines are a solo air for the Sorceress. Does this mean that the score represents a wholesale revision of Purcell's original composition? Again it must be emphasized that such a conclusion appears totally unwarranted, and in this case it is possible to argue against the reading in the libretto and playbook on the basis of the seventh line, which is completely garbled: 'Elisas ruin'ed, ho, ho, ho, next motion'. In the score it becomes 'Eliza's ruin'd, ho, ho, ho' (end of witches' dialogue) and 'Our next motion . . .' (beginning of the Sorceress's song). The text in the musical source, therefore, is the only one that is coherent, and there is no reason to doubt the authenticity of the musical setting. Thus, the 1689 libretto must once again be inaccurate or, once again, Purcell deliberately altered the original text for the sake of musical variety. In either case, however, the version in the 1689 libretto was perpetuated in 1700; only the much later musical sources offer the correct reading.

Even when all three sources differ, the Tenbury manuscript sometimes seems to provide the correct reading. At least, it is impossible to prove the musical source is corrupt in these cases. For example, the opening lines of Act III ('Come away, fellow sailors') are assigned in the libretto to the chorus only; in the 1700 playbook they are given to the Sorceress (!) only. Of these, the first is dramatically possible, the second more difficult, unless one imagines the Sorceress disguised as a sailor.[7] It is most likely, however, that Purcell intended the lines to be sung first by a single sailor and then repeated by chorus, just as they are set in the Tenbury score. Not only is this distribution of lines, with a solo followed by choral repetition, a regular feature of Purcell's music, but both the 1689 and 1700 texts have shown themselves to be unreliable in similar situations where a soloist is answered by chorus. That is, 'Harm's our delight' is not designated for chorus, the choral repetition of 'Thanks to these lonesome vales' is inaccurately represented, and the choral repetition of 'Haste, haste to town' is lacking altogether in 1689. With 'Come away, fellow Sailors', Purcell probably changed Tate's text. In this case the 1700 playbook may offer what was a special variant in that performance, or simply a unique printing error.

The same set of conclusions obtains in a very similar situation also concerning the role of the Sorceress. In Act II, scene i, the libretto assigns the Sorceress all of the following lines:

> The *Trojan* Prince you know is bound
> By Fate to seek *Italian* Ground.
> The Queen and He are now in Chase,
> Hark, how the cry comes on apace.
> But when they've done, my trusty Elf
> In Form of *Mercury* himself,
> As sent from *Jove* shall chide his stay,
> And charge him Sail to Night with all his Fleet away.

---

[7] Curtis Price discusses this possibility in *Henry Purcell*, 254.

Ho, ho, ho, ho, etc.
But e're we this perform,
We'l Conjure for a Storm.
To Mar their Hunting Sport,
And drive 'em back to Court.

The laughter in the ninth line, however, must clearly be for the chorus—parallel to the laughing chorus that occurs just before this speech. Thus the correction is made in the 1700 playbook and in the musical sources, where the 'ho's' are indeed set for chorus. The quatrain following the laughing chorus, however, presents a more serious problem.

In 1700 these lines are not assigned to the Sorceress alone, but, as an apparent duet, to her and a witch. In the Tenbury manuscript this section is indeed a duet, but it is sung by the first and second witches with no participation by the Sorceress. All three designations are supportable dramatically, but because two of the sources identify the lines as a duet, and, of course, the setting is a duet, this change from the libretto can be accepted. Perhaps it is another Purcellian improvement for musical variety. Although there is no absolute way of determining which of the two designations for the duet is authentic, the use of two witches, as in the Tenbury manuscript, seems to fit the text better; the storm will be the witches' small addition to the Sorceress's grand plan. In Tenbury, the entry of the two witches is prepared by giving the first witch the fourth line, 'Hark, how the cry comes on apace', as well.

In all of the situations discussed so far, it has been argued that the 1689 libretto either contained errors or was altered by Purcell. In these cases, the authenticity of the Tenbury manuscript has been accepted because the dramatic result is substantially improved and because the musical setting is both coherent and fits what we know of Purcell's compositional practices. In other cases, however, the Tenbury manuscript clearly lacks authenticity, and sometimes this can be argued from the musical setting itself.

In Act I, after Dido speaks of her love for Aeneas in the quatrain beginning, 'Whence could so much virtue spring?', the 1689 libretto and the 1700 playbook both divide the following quatrain between Belinda and the Second Woman.

BELINDA. A Tale so strong and full of woe,
  Might melt the rocks as well as you.
SECOND WOMAN. What stubborn heart unmoved could see,
  Such Distress, such Piety.

Although the score gives the entire quatrain to Belinda, the music itself denies the validity of this designation. Dido sings her lines entirely in C minor and ends with a strong cadence. Belinda's lines effect a modulation to the minor dominant (G) and also cadence strongly. The next lines (starting with 'What stubborn heart') begin abruptly in the new key of E flat (the relative major of C minor). The strong cadence coming in the middle of the quatrain and the clear use of two contrasting key areas indicate a separation of the four lines of verse into two distinct couplets matching the designations of the earlier textual sources that split these four lines between two singers. In the musical settings of the lines preceding and following this text, all sung completely by Dido, there are no internal, interruptive cadences, and there is continuity in the harmony.

In this case, the Tenbury manuscript gave more text to Belinda than was originally intended. The situation occurs repeatedly throughout the score. In Act I, the 1689 libretto and the 1700 playbook both assign 'The greatest blessing fate can give' to the Second Woman, not Belinda, and they assign the lead-in to the chorus 'Haste, haste to town' in Act II to Dido rather than Belinda. It seems, in fact, that the Tenbury score represents a version of the original in which Belinda's part was raised in stature by the addition of lines intended for other female charac-ters. Although there is nothing 'wrong' with these designations, the dramatic situations often make them less suitable than those offered in the earlier texts.

Just before 'Haste, haste to town', it had been Dido who first saw the clouds and heard the thunder. If she herself then sings 'Haste, haste to town', urging her court to hurry away, she can exit quickly but with authority, and leave Aeneas on stage for his encounter with the Spirit. This is better than having Belinda suddenly function to separate the loving couple after all her matchmaking in Act I. In the other cases, the increased use of the Second Woman helps prepare for her important solo in Act II ('Oft she visits') that otherwise seems out of place. Thus, on the basis of the dramatic situation in 'Haste, haste to town', the musical situation in 'Whence could so much virtue spring', and the proper balance among the characters throughout, it seems best in all these 'Belinda' cases to follow the earlier printed texts, not the musical scores.

Other changes can be attributed directly to the 1700 performance. For example, the dance described in 1689 as 'Eccho Dance. Inchanteress and Fairies' becomes thereafter 'Echo Dance of Furies'. The furies here are not a simple misreading of fairies, but, rather, they illustrate the apparent desire for added spectacle in the professional production of *Dido* in 1700. Indeed, the enthusiasm for spectacle led the adapter to reverse the scenes in Act II so that the scene with the 'furies' would end the act,[8] and it should be noted that the shifting of spectacular scenes to the ends of acts was not an uncommon adaptation in the conversion of various works into dramatic operas. For example, when the Restoration adaptation of Shakespeare's *The Tempest* by Sir William Davenant and John Dryden (1670) was transformed into a dramatic opera in 1674, perhaps by Thomas Shadwell, one of the major changes was the shifting of the four scenes in Act II so that the first scene, which ends with a masque of devils, could conclude the act. In the opera, then, scenes iii and iv of Dryden's Act II precede scene i (which ends Shadwell's Act II) and scene ii (which begins Shadwell's Act III). That is, Dryden's II (1–2–3–4) becomes in the operatic adaptation II (3–4–1) III (2–). The similarity to the shifting of scenes in *Dido* for the same reason is obvious. Thus, although *Measure for Measure* may have included furies, it is more than likely that the girls of Josias Priest's Boarding School in Chelsea portrayed fairies.

In a similar situation in Act III, the 1689 libretto (see Plate 3) calls for the following:

> Jack of the Lanthorn leads the Spaniards out of their way among the Inchanteresses. A Dance.

In the manner of a comic diversion from the main plot, this direction indicates a lightening of mood immediately before the final denouement. The witches have just sung 'Elissa dyes to Night, and Carthage Flames to Morrow', and following the

[8] Eric Walter White, 'New Light on *Dido and Aeneas*', in *Henry Purcell (1659–1695): Essays on his Music*, 23–4, mentions the added spectacle desired in theatrical productions, but he does not refer to the change from 'fairies' to 'furies'.

dance Aeneas and Dido will have their final confrontation,
bringing on all that the witches have predicted. But first a
nightwatchman enters leading a group of bewildered Spanish
sailors to their ships (trade between Carthage and Spain was
known to have been active). By 1700, however, the entire
direction was omitted in favour of 'A dance of wizards and
witches', which in the score becomes simply 'The Witches
Dance'. Once again the need in the 1700 production for the
spectacular appears to have encroached upon the simplicity of the
original, and the change stuck. In these cases, only the 1689
libretto seems to preserve the version originally performed.

Finally, the 1700 textbook offers a slightly different version of
the opera's last chorus, which in 1689 and Tenbury is given as
follows:

> With drooping Wings you *Cupids* come,
> To scatter Roses on her Tomb.
> Soft and Gentle as her Heart,
> Keep here your Watch and never part.

In 1700 the second line is omitted, as is the stage direction '*Cupids*
appear in the Clouds o're her Tomb'. Price argues that the
references to Dido's tomb are deliberately eliminated because in
this version Dido does not die.[9] He postulates that the change was
due in part to the dramatic position of the opera within Shakespeare's *Measure for Measure* and also to the likelihood that the
same actress played both Dido in the opera and Isabella in the
play.[10] Price may well be correct, although the musical sources all
preserve the final chorus as it appears in the 1689 libretto, leaving
open the possibility that the reading in the 1700 playbook is
simply an error of omission. And one wants to ask why these
funereal references would need to be omitted at all if, as Price also
argues, Tate's original libretto leaves the Queen 'to linger on the
point of death' without dying. Price's argument about the
possible revision of this scene in the 1700 version only emphasizes
that in 1689 both the text and music clearly indicate that Dido
dies.

   [9] Price, *Henry Purcell*, 262.
   [10] Curtis Price, 'The Allegorical Designs of *Dido and Aeneas*', a paper delivered to the
American Musicological Society Annual Meeting (Ann Arbor, 1982), and Price, *Henry
Purcell*, 238, n. 22.

This examination of the relatively small textual discrepancies among the three primary sources illustrates that no one text is definitive, but that careful consideration of the variants may result in a reconstruction of Purcell's original text using readings from all three. Each situation has needed to be judged individually on its own merits. That is, where the 1689 libretto is in error, the proper reading may be found as early as 1700. Sometimes, however, the error is perpetuated in 1700 and the correct form found only in the musical score. Sometimes the 1689 libretto appears to have been altered by Purcell before the first performance for musical variety; in most, but not all of these cases, the preferred reading is given in 1700. In other cases, where the 1689 libretto is correct, changes have been made in 1700; these have sometimes been perpetuated, in which cases one must return to the 1689 libretto for the correct reading. Sometimes the 1700 playbook includes a special version not repeated elsewhere, and sometimes changes (for example, to Belinda's role) seem to have been made after 1700. In sum, the examination of textual variants illustrates an erratic pattern of authenticity. It is important to remember this finding when examining the major formal discrepancies among the three primary sources.

5

The Tenbury Manuscript: Omissions
Prologue

The 1689 libretto contains a mythological Prologue (the beginning of which is shown in Plate 2) that is about the length of a
single act of the opera. It mainly concerns Phoebus (Apollo) and
Venus (who can be seen as allegorical representations of the new
English monarchs, William and Mary) and ends with a pastoral
ode to spring, which suits the time when the opera was first
performed. Such allegorical Prologues were traditionally considered entirely separable from the main body of the drama—the
best example of this being the Prologue that Dryden wrote for his
dramatic opera *King Arthur*, which was detached, expanded, and
produced on its own as a musically continuous opera entitled
Albion and Albanius. The Prologue of *Dido and Aeneas* is no more
necessary to the production of that opera than *Albion and Albanius*
was to *King Arthur*.

In the production of *Dido* in 1700, the Prologue was included as
the final musical entertainment, following Act III. In this position
it was meant to fulfil the need for a concluding mythological
masque, something that had been traditional since Shakespeare
had begun to use masques in his plays, as for example the 'Masque
of Hymen' at the end of *As You Like It*, the 'sun-burnt sicklemen'
introduced by Juno and Iris in the fourth act of *The Tempest*, and
even, perhaps, the comic rendition of Pyramus and Thisbe by
Bottom and his friends at the end of *A Midsummer Night's Dream*,
which is introduced by Theseus asking, 'What masques? what
dances shall we have?' Such concluding masques were particularly
popular in Restoration dramatic opera and plays. In the 1674
musical adaptation of *The Tempest* a long masque, 'The Masque
of Neptune and Amphitrite', is appended to the final act. In the
1690 adaptation of Fletcher's play *The Prophetess* (which was
retitled *Dioclesian*) with music by Purcell, the most sustained

58

stretch of music by far is the concluding masque. Similarly, in
the 1699 adaptation of Fletcher's *The Island Princess*, a masque
presenting a view of courtship in each of the four seasons of life is
appended. That is, the concluding masque, comprising allegorical
or pastoral characters, was typical of dramatic opera; using the
Prologue of *Dido* in this way was an ingenious solution to one of
the problems that arose in the adaptation of this work into that
form.

Despite its new position, the allegorical meaning of the Prologue of *Dido and Aeneas* was not abandoned. Although no longer
so timely, for Mary had been dead for six years and the new
production did not occur in spring, it nevertheless continued to
praise William, and changes were made in the text to reflect both
the season and the current political situation. The pastoral ending
was shortened and moved to an earlier point in the masque, and a
new ending, consisting of a dialogue between Mars and Peace
appended. At the time of this production William had been
urging the creation of a large military force to combat the French
claims in Spain. The English, however, were weary of war and
thus Parliament refused William's requests, remembering no
doubt that the king had never succeeded as a military leader. The
new ending of the Prologue-masque seems to refer to this
directly:

> PEACE: 'Tis time for War's alarms to cease,
> And Heroes crown'd with spoils,
> Enjoy the Harvest of their toils,
> And reap the happy Fruits of Peace.
>
> . . . .
>
> Wherefore must the Warriour be
> To restless Tasks assign'd,
> Give others those delights which he
> Must never hope to find.
>
> . . . .
>
> Must he with endless toils be prest,
> Nor with repose himself be blest,
> Who gives the weary Nations rest.
>
> . . . .
>
> CHORUS: Since it is decreed that Wars should cease,
> Let's all agree to welcome Peace.

Neither the 1689 or 1700 version of the Prologue appears in
Tenbury or in any of the later musical sources, and it is reasonable

to suppose that by 1704, when *Dido* was next performed after 1700, that this part of the opera was dropped. King William had died in 1702, and it would have been impossible to make any of the text appropriate to Queen Anne. Nevertheless the opera itself was still performed, for it did not depend upon an allegorical interpretation that was no longer timely, nor did it depend on the use of the Prologue, which had never been an integral part of the drama. There is no reason to assume, however, that Purcell did not set this text for the first performance in 1689. Indeed, both Curtis Price and Margaret Laurie have recently proposed that an instrumental movement in G minor preserved in the Royal College of Music, London, and entitled 'Overture in Mr P Opera' might be the original overture to the Prologue of *Dido*.[11] Unfortunately, as Price points out, there is currently not sufficient evidence to prove such an hypothesis. In sum, the Prologue to *Dido and Aeneas* must be counted among Purcell's lost works.

It appears that Purcell and Tate gave careful thought to this section being set to music, for they apparently correlated the number of characters and possible voice ranges in the Prologue and the opera.

Venus	Dido
Phoebus	Aeneas
Spring	Belinda
2 Nereids	2 Witches
Shepherdesses	Second Woman and Spirit
Country Shepherdess	Sorceress
Country Shepherd	Sailor

Although the exact relations between characters might have been different (for example, Belinda might have played the Country Shepherdess, and the Sorceress, Spring), the exact parity in roles points to equality in vocal ranges. In both the Prologue and opera, there are two male roles (Aeneas/Phoebus and Sailor/Shepherd), there is one set of paired voices (Nereids and Witches), and there is a single couple. The voice ranges that have become commonly associated with these roles, however, cannot be found in any single, surviving musical source.

We are accustomed to hearing Aeneas as a second tenor or high baritone, the Sailor as a tenor, and all the female parts (including

[11] Price, *Henry Purcell*, 245; Margaret Laurie, 'Tempest', 45, n. 8.

the Spirit) as treble. However, the role of the Sailor is only given in tenor clef in the Academy sources, where Belinda's role (Anna) is in alto clef and the Sorceress's role is in bass clef. As the roles of the Sailor, Sorceress, and Belinda are all in treble clef in Tenbury and Tatton Park, the assumption has been that these parts were transposed down to achieve greater vocal variety in the late eighteenth-century productions. This implies that even the Sailor was played by a female in 1689, and it leads one to question whether the role of Aeneas might not also have been transposed later. There is, however, no way to determine definitively the original vocal range of either of the male characters as an original score is lacking and we do not have a cast list from 1689. All that can be said with assurance is that the female characters in 1689 were certainly all trebles.

We also do not know who sang in *Dido and Aeneas* in 1700, except for the existence of a publication of 'The Saylors Song, set by Mr Purcell, Sung by Mr Wiltshire in the Play call'd "Measure for Measure"'.[12] As John Wiltshire was a tenor, this implies that at least by 1700 the Sailor was sung in that range, even though the song was published in the treble clef. The rubric in the 1700 playbook that this song be sung by the Sorceress may indicate, however, that Mr Wiltshire sang that role and the Sailor's part was eliminated. It is more likely, however, since the published song is entitled 'The Saylors Song', that Mr Wiltshire sang the Sailor and that the role designation in the playbook for this song is an error.

In the 1704 productions the Prologue was eliminated and the 'masque of Mars and Venus' by John Eccles and Godfrey Finger apparently substituted for it. The correlation of parts between this masque and Purcell's opera is at least as interesting as with the Prologue, especially as the original singers' names and the music are preserved.[13] The singing roles of *Mars and Venus* call for one

[12] Preserved in the Bodleian Library, Oxford, Mus. I. *c.* 73.

[13] A contemporary libretto (with the original cast list) of *Mars and Venus* by Pierre Motteux (London, 1696) is preserved in Special Collections of Regenstein Library, University of Chicago. Copies of *Single Songs and Dialogues in the Musical Play of Mars and Venus* (London: J. Heptinstall, 1696) survive in the British Library and Royal College of Music, London, and the Library of Congress, Washington, D.C.. In the libretto the part of Cupid is assigned to Jemmy Laroche (b. 1688); the printed score shows his range to be from d' to g". Mars is assigned to the well-known bass John Bowman; except for the dialogue in Act III, where Mars's part is printed in treble clef, this role is given in the bass clef. Vulcan was played by John Reading; this part is also given in bass clef in the printed

boy, three men, and five women. An attempted comparison with
Purcell's opera is instructive.

Cupid	(boy)	Spirit
Mars	(bass)	Aeneas
Vulcan	(bass)	?
Gallus	(tenor)	Sailor
Venus	(soprano)	Dido
2 Graces	(sopranos)	2 Witches
Hora (Venus's attendant)		
	(soprano)	Belinda
Jealousy	(soprano)	Sorceress
?		Second Woman

Apparently there is one less woman in the masque than called for
in the opera and one extra bass. It is possible, however, that the
additional bass sang the Sorceress's role (for this role was sung by
a bass in the Academy performances), and the woman who
played Jealousy sang the Second Woman. It is also possible that
the number of solo female parts was reduced to five by the
elimination of the role of the Second Woman. Although on the
surface this latter theory may seem the more unlikely, it coincides
with the version of the opera that is preserved in the Tenbury
manuscript, where most of the lines of the Second Woman and
some lines of Dido are reassigned to Belinda.

The following conclusions may thus be drawn about vocal
ranges in *Dido*. The role of Aeneas was sung by a male baritone at
least by 1704, if not earlier, and this range is preserved in all
surviving manuscripts. The role of the Sailor was probably sung
by a tenor in both 1700 and 1704, if not also in 1689, despite the
fact that this role is given in the treble clef in both the Tenbury
and Tatton Park manuscripts; all later sources place the role in the
tenor clef. Although circumstantial evidence might lead to the
conclusion that the Sorceress was played by a male voice in both
1700 and 1704, this hypothesis cannot be strongly supported; the
Academy manuscripts are the first to place the role of the

---

score. The part of Gallas was played by Mr (James?) Lee, but the libretto states that the part
was 'design'd for Mr Dogget'; no music for this role appears in the printed score, but
Dogget was a well-known actor/singer who sang in the tenor range. Venus was played by
Mrs Bracegirdle, the two graces by Mrs Hodgson and Mrs Ayliff, Hora by Mrs Perrin, and
Jealously by Mrs Hudson; the surviving music for all these parts is in the treble clef and of
approximately the same range (d' to g").

Sorceress in the bass clef. By 1704 the role of the Spirit was taken by a boy treble, and the singers' names given in the Folger manuscript indicate that this tradition continued.[14] The ranges of the other roles have never come into question.

By comparing the roles in *Dido and Aeneas* to the roles in the Prologue, by tracing the history of the Prologue in 1700, and by recognizing the substitution of the masque of *Mars and Venus* for the Prologue in 1704, it becomes possible to pin-point the origin of the musical version preserved in the Tenbury manuscript more closely. As stated above, the Tenbury score seems to represent a performance in which Belinda's role was expanded primarily at the expense of the Second Woman. In fact, by giving either Dido or Belinda the second act song, 'Oft she visits', the role can be eliminated, leaving five female singers, two of whom (the two witches) regularly sing together. This matches the requirements for female singers in *Mars and Venus* exactly, and it implies that *Dido* was altered in 1704 to suit the requirements of a specific company. Because it also lacks the Prologue, and the role of the Second Woman is reduced to the point where it need not exist, the Tenbury manuscript appears to reflect most closely the 1704 productions.[15]

[14] In the Folger manuscript the part of the Spirit is identified with the name Edward Mays; I presume this refers to a boy treble rather than a countertenor or an implication that the role was transposed. Adult singers are usually identified by last name only. In a recent article, Curtis Price and Irena Cholij ('Dido's Bass Sorceress', *The Musical Times*, cxxvii [1986], 615–18) have argued that the Sorceress was possibly played by a bass from the time of the first production and have offered evidence that this was at least the case in 1700 based on prompter's notes that survive in the Folger Library copy of the *Measure for Measure* playbook. As has been shown here, a comparison of the casts of *Mars and Venus* with *Dido and Aeneas* offers evidence that the Sorceress was possibly sung by a bass in 1704. A comparison of the casts of the original Prologue with *Dido and Aeneas*, however, argues for a woman in the role of the Sorceress in 1689. This is corroborated by the Tenbury and Tatton Park manuscripts, which, although copied *c.*1780, do not represent the concert versions of that period and presumably represent earlier versions. As the Sorceress's role is given in treble clef for both sources, it is difficult to argue for the bass range in any early version, except, perhaps, 1700. The state of both manuscripts has been shown most likely to reflect the 1704 performances, which were primarily based on the 1689 performance. There would be no reason for this role not to have been preserved in bass clef, as was Aeneas's in *Dido*, Mars's and Vulcan's in *Mars and Venus*, and other bass roles from this period, if the role had been performed by a bass without exception.

[15] This conclusion is also suggested by Margaret Laurie, ed. *Dido and Aeneas*, Preface, ix, and by E.W. White, 'New Light', 17.

Choruses and Dances

The 1689 libretto contains indications for eleven dances in the three acts of the opera, as follows:

Act I: 1. Dance this cho. The baske
          2. A dance Gittars chacony
          3. The Triumphing Dance
Act II: 4. Enter two drunken sailors, a Dance
          5. Eccho Dance
          6. Gitter [sic] ground a Dance
          7. A dance by Dido's Women to Entertain Aeneas
          8. The Groves Dance
Act III: 9. The Saylors Dance
          10. Jack of the Lanthorn . . . A Dance
          11. Cupids Dance

In 1700 only six dances are indicated: The Baske, The Triumphing Dance, Echo Dance (now for furies, not fairies), The Groves Dance, The Saylors Dance, and a Dance for the Wizards and Witches to replace the Jack of Lanthorn Dance. By the time of the Tenbury manuscript, only four dances are given in the musical score: The Triumphing Dance, Echo Dance of Furies, The Saylors Dance, and The Witches Dance. It would appear at first glance that at each revision the number of dances was reduced, but a careful study of the score and libretto illustrates that this is probably not the case at all.

The very first dance, The Baske, gives an indication of what has happened, for the specific instruction is given in both 1689 and 1700 to 'dance this chorus', referring to 'Fear no danger', which movement not only contains strong dance rhythms throughout but is constructed in the dance pattern of a rondo. Thus, The Baske was undoubtedly danced during the choral repetition of 'Fear no danger'. That is, The Baske was never set as a separate dance movement, and, despite the fact that this dance is not indicated in the score, no movement has been omitted. By applying this solution to other situations, still more dances can be uncovered.

The hunting scene in Act II opens with a series of pantomimes. The comparative analysis of the *Dido* libretto and Tate's play *Brutus of Alba* has shown that the chorus 'Thanks to these lonesome vales', which is strongly rhythmical and in repeated binary dance form, accompanies the ritual post-hunt worship of Diana, after which the 'masque' consists of a song by the Second Woman who relates the story of Diana and Actaeon; this concludes with a long instrumental postlude continuing the ground bass of the song, with the upper strings following the repetitive pattern AABCC. Although unnotated in the score, this postlude undoubtedly accompanied the 'dance by Dido's Women to Entertain Aeneas'.

In the first scene of the second act, the libretto includes the direction: 'Enter two Drunken Sailors. A Dance'. Immediately following is the duet 'But ere we this perform' in very fast duple metre and in repeated binary form—the only piece in the opera other than 'Thanks to these lonesome vales' to take this form. It is musically appropriate for dancing, and it seems entirely possible that the sailors could enter at the point indicated, dancing to this duet that tells of the control the witches have over their fate.

Cupids Dance follows the final chorus, 'With drooping wings' and apparently ends the opera, except that the manuscripts contain no separate music for it. The chorus, however, is enclosed in repeat marks. It seems unlikely that this movement should be sung in its entirety twice, but if it is repeated instrumentally, it could well represent the 'lost' music for the Cupids Dance.[16] Although the music of this chorus is not obviously in dance style, it might accompany the pantomimed action of Cupids scattering roses on Dido's tomb. That is, whether or not the chorus is meant to accompany it, the dance called for here is clearly not intended to be a typical court or figure dance, and while the music itself is not inherently dance-like, its formal structure, which includes many repetitions, appears appropriate for repeated and rhythmical action; its overall plan is AA' B CC' D EE'.

This process of finding dances in texted movements of *Dido* reveals two important musical aspects of the score; first, that there are two different kinds of choruses, and, second, that there are two different kinds of dances. That is, the choruses may be danced or not, and the dances may be formal or pantomimed. The danced choruses can be distinguished from the others by their

---

[16] This interpretation is suggested in the editions of this author and Margaret Laurie.

regular rhythmic and metric structure, by their repetitive form, by relatively simple textures, and substantive length. Many or all of these qualities characterize 'Thanks to these lonesome vales', 'Fear no danger', and 'With drooping wings', as well as the duet 'But ere we this perform'. On the other hand, 'Cupid only throws the dart' and 'Great minds against themselves conspire' contain intricate contrapuntal writing, are through-composed without the repetition of distinct sections, have irregular phrase structure, and are very short. In all respects they are unsuited to dancing of either a free or formal type. 'When monarchs unite' and 'Harm's our delight' are so short as to preclude dancing. The laughing choruses and 'Haste, haste to town' are contrapuntal throughout. 'Banish sorrow, banish care' is contrapuntal in part, short, and has an irregular phrase structure. In sum, none of these choruses is as obviously suitable for dancing as those that because of their position within the libretto would seem to be used as dances, and the distinctions in musical style tend to corroborate the implications of the text.

The dances are also of two types: those that represent free pantomimes and those that are formal with patterned and regular steps. To take obvious examples, The Baske ('Fear no danger') is clearly of the formal category, whereas the Jack of Lanthorn dance is a pantomime. The Baske has a strongly accented rhythmic and metric pattern, a constant tempo, and is constructed in regular eight-bar phrases with much repetition (AABACA). The Jack of Lanthorn dance, on the other hand, consists of three sections of differing lengths, different tempos, and different metres; the rhythmic patterns, especially in the first section, are odd and inconsistent. No regular dance could be performed to such an accompaniment. Cupids Dance is probably also of this type, as is, undoubtedly, the dance of the Two Drunken Sailors. Another obvious candidate for a pantomimed dance is the Echo Dance of the fairies/furies, which with its short, echoed phrases seems to call out for irregular movements and poses. Indeed, even the musical echoes of this dance are distorted. Although the top melodic line 'echoes' correctly, the bass and inner parts are altered to create dissonances lacking in the original. These distortions characterize the dancers, and they add to the musical irregularity of a movement that already lacks any regular rhythmic pattern, phrase structure, or sectional repetition (Example 1).

Example 1: Echo Dance, first echo (as edited by the author)

Besides The Baske, the other patterned dances in *Dido* include The Triumphing Dance, based on a ground bass of four bars that imposes regular phrase structure upon the movement. The 'Dance to entertain Aeneas' is also constructed over a four-bar ground, and, like The Triumphing Dance, includes distinct melodic repetition as well. And The Saylors Dance, constructed out of two eight-bar phrases, each repeated, also contains very strongly accented and regular rhythmic patterns.

The freer dance style derives historically from the antimasques of the pre-Commonwealth court masque, which, like the panto-mimed dances in *Dido*, are irregular in form and usually comic (Two Drunken Sailors, Jack of Lanthorn), grotesque (Eccho Dance), or elfin (Cupids Dance). The more formal dances are based on the entry dances of the masquers, which were regular in form and accompanied standard dance patterns. Thus the duality of style as well as the styles themselves in the dances of *Dido* have strong English antecedents in the masque.[17]

The two dances for guitar (gittar) that are indicated in the libretto (Act I and Act II) were almost certainly improvised, and for this reason were not included in the orchestral score. In both cases, according to the directions given in the libretto, the dances were based on a repeated harmonic pattern; the first dance calls for a chaconne bass, the second for an unnamed ground. It seems unlikely, however, that these dances belong to the formal cate-gory, in part on account of their presumed improvisatory nature. Furthermore, they both come at places in the drama where music is needed to accompany a movement or action. The first, occurring just after Belinda's 'Pursue thy conquest, Love', could accompany a pantomime indicating Dido's acceptance of Aeneas

---

[17] See the antimasque and entry dances in Andrew Sabol, *Four Hundred Songs and Dances from the Stuart Masque* (Providence, R.I., 1963), and see below, Part II, Chapter 7, for a further discussion of masques and antimasques.

as a suitor and thus fill in a gap in the story line of the opera. The second, coming between 'Thanks to these lonesome vales' and 'Oft she visits', serves as a link between the Diana worship and the entertainment; perhaps it simply accompanies the repositioning of the characters on stage. Thus both of these dances, which can easily be added to modern productions, can be performed as pantomimes, although formal dances would not be inappropriate given the repetitive bass structures.

The only dance left unaccounted for, then, is The Groves Dance at the end of Act II, and the situation is complicated by the fact that the preceding chorus, 'Then since our charms have sped', which might have functioned as the dance music, is lacking as well. The question that arises is whether this double omission was original, occurring at the time of the first performance, a variant introduced in a later version, or simply an accident in the transmission of the score. The answer possibly lies in the overall layout of the opera.

1. Portrait of Henry Purcell in black chalk, attributed to Godfrey Kneller (1646–1723) and thought to have been drawn from life. The portrait once belonged to Charles Burney.

AN OPERA

Perform'd at

Mr. JOSIAS PRIEST's Boarding-School at
CHELSEY.

By Young Gentlewomen.

The Words Made by Mr. NAT. TATE.

The Musick Compos'd by Mr. Henry Purcell.

The PROLOGUE.

Phœbus Rises in the Chariot,
Over the Sea, The *Nereids* out of the Sea.

Phœbus,	FRom *Aurora*'s Spicy Bed, *Phœbus* rears his Sacred Head. His Coursers Advancing, Curvetting and Prancing.
1. *Nereid,*	*Phœbus* strives in vain to Tame 'em, With *Ambrosia* Fed too high.
2. *Nereid,*	*Phœbus* ought not now to blame 'em, Wild and eager to Survey The fairest Pageant of the Sea.
Phœbus, Cho.	*Tritons* and *Nereids* come pay your Devotion To the New rising Star of the Ocean.

Venus Descends in her Chariot,
The *Tritons* out of the Sea.
The *Tritons* Dance.

Nereid.	Look down ye Orbs and See A New Divinity.
Phœ.	Whose Lustre does Out-Shine Your fainter Beams, and half Eclipses mine, Give *Phœbus* leave to Prophecy. *Phœbus* all Events can see. Ten Thousand Thousand Harmes, From such prevailing Charmes, To Gods and Men must instantly Ensue.
Cho.	And if the Deity's above, Are *Victims* of the powers of Love, What must wretched Mortals do.
Venus)	Fear not *Phœbus*, fear not me, A harmless Deity.

A   These

---

2. *Dido and Aeneas*, first page of 1689 libretto, showing author, composer, and
performance details, in addition to the beginning of the Prologue.

But ah ! what Language can I try,
My Injured Queen to pacify.
No fooner fhe refignes her Heart,
But from her Armes I'm forc't to part.
How can fo hard a Fate be took,
One Night enjoy'd, the next forfook.
Your be the blame, ye Gods, for I
Obey your will - but with more Eafe cou'd dye,
> *The Sorcerefs and her Inchanterefs.*

Cho.
Then fince our Charmes have Sped,
A Merry Dance be Led.
By the Nymphs of *Carthage* to pleafe us,
They fhall all Dance to eafe us.
A Dance that fhall make the Spheres to wonder,
Rending thofe fair Groves afunder.
> *The Groves Dance.*

ACT the Third,

Scene the Ships.

Enter the Saylors.

The Sorcerefs and her Inchanterefs.

Cho.
COme away, fellow Saylors your Anchors be
Time and Tide will admit no delaying. (weighing
Take a Bouze fhort leave of your Nymphs on the Shore,
And Silence their Morning,
VVith Vows of teturning.
But never intending to Vifit them more.
> *The Saylors Dance.*

Sorc.
See the Flags and Streamers Curling,
Anchors weighing, Sails unfurling.
Phœbus pale deluding Beames,
Guilding more deceitful Streams.
> Our Plot has took,
> The Queen forfook, ho, ho, ho.
Elifa ruin'd, ho, ho, ho, next Motion,
Muft be to ftorme her Lover on the Ocean.
From the Ruines of others our pleafure we borrow,
Elifa bleeds to Night, and *Carthage* Flames tomorrow.

Cho.
Deftruction our delight, delight our greateft Sorrow,
Elifa dyes to Night, and *Carthage* Flames to Morrow,
> § Jack of the Lanthorn *leads the* Spaniards
> *out of their way among the Inchanterefses.*
> *A Dance.*

B 2   Enter

---

3. *Dido and Aeneas,* 1689 libretto, end of Act II, showing Aeneas's monologue followed by a chorus and dance for the witches, and beginning of Act III, giving the Sorceress's speech.

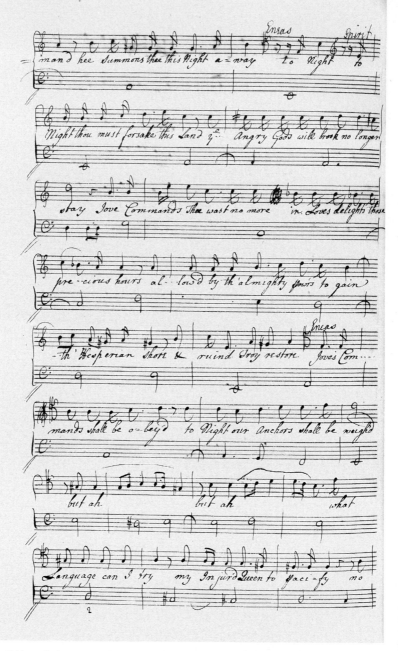

4. *Dido and Aeneas*, Tenbury manuscript, showing Aeneas's monologue and the end of Act II.

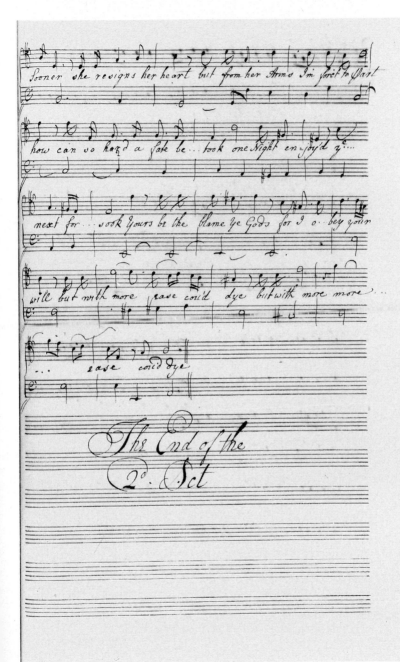

Sooner she resigns her heart but from her Arms I'm forc't to part

how can so hard a fate be...took one Night enjoy'd y...

next for...sook Yours be the blame Ye Gods for I o..bey your

will but with more ease could dye but with more more...

...ease could dye

The End of the
2d Act

Esca. He's grown Thoughtful, I hope he's won.

Ang. Can Virtue win us more to Vice, than Vice?

> Oh! fie! fie! fie! What doſt thou *Angelo*?
> Is it her Virtue, that thou lov'ſt? oh! no!
> Thou falſe and deluding Guide, who in Diſguiſe
> Of Virtues ſhape, leadſt us thro' Heav'n to Hell!
> No Vicious Beauty cou'd with Practis'd Art,   *[aſide.*
> Subdue my Heart like Virgin Innocence.
> I'll think no more on't, but with Muſick chaſe
> Away the Guilty Image.
> Muſick they ſay can Calm the ruffled Soul,
> I'm ſure a mighty Tempeſt ruffles mine.

My Lord, if your Diverſions now are ready
I am diſpos'd to ſee 'em.

Eſc. Pleaſe you to ſit, they wait but your Command.

Luc. Begin the *Opera*, the Deputy attends.   They all ſit

The LOVES of *Dido* and *Æneas*, a MASK, in Four MUSICAL ENTERTAINMENTS.

The Firſt Entertainment.

Enter QUEEN DIDO, Belinda, *and* Train.

Belinda *SINGS.*

Bel. SHake the Cloud from off your Brow,
> Fate your Wiſhes does Allow;
> Empire Growing,
> Pleaſures Flowing;
> Fortune Smiles, and ſo ſhou'd you,
> Shake the Cloud from off your Brow.

Cho. Baniſh Sorrow, Baniſh Care,
> Grief ſhou'd ne're approach the Fair.

Dido. Ah! Belinda I am preſt,
> With Torment not to be Confeſt:
> Peace and I are ſtrangers grown,
> I languiſh till my Grief is known,
> Yet wou'd not have it Gueſt.

Bel. Grief Encreaſing, by Concealing.

Dido. Mine admits of no Revealing.

Bel. Then let me ſpeak, the Trojan gueſt,
> Into your Tender Thoughts has preſt.

2 Woman. The greateſt Bleſſing Fate can give,
> Our Carthage to ſecure, and Troy revive.

Cho. When Monarchs unite, how happy their State.
> They Triumph at once or'e their Foes and their Fate.

Dido. *Whence*

---

5. *Measure for Measure,* 1700 playbook, beginning of masque, *The Loves of Dido and Aeneas.*

Selected by PETER STAPEL, Efq.

Thurfday, February 22d, 1787.

Academy of Ancient Mufic.

A C T I.

OVERTURE, PHARAMOND	—	*Handel.*
MADRIGAL. Chlori fon fido	—	*Stradella.*
DUET. Ceafe thy Anguifh	—	*Handel.*
ANTHEM. I heard a great Voice		*Dr. Cooke.*
GLEE. When Sappho tun'd	—	*Danby.*
MOTETT. Domine ad adjuvandum		*Pergolefi.*

A C T II.

CONCERTO 3d, Op. 4ta.	——	*Avifon.*
GLEE. Hark! the Lark	——	*Dr. Cooke.*
MASQUE. Dido and Æneas	—	*Purcell.*
Full ANTHEM. My Heart is inditing		*Handel.*

6. Academy of Ancient Music, programme for 22 February 1787.

7. *Dido and Aeneas*, Academy version, Aeneas's monologue.

Night thou must forsake this land the angry Gods will brook no

longer stay   Jove commands thee waste no more in Love's delights those

precious hours   allow'd by the Almighty pow'rs to gain   the Latian,

shore   and ruin'd Troy restore.   Æneas

Jove's commands must be o-

bey'd   to night   our   Anchors shall be weigh'd.

Ah! ah! ah! Belinda, a fingle SONG.

8. 'Ah, Belinda', from *Orpheus Britannicus*, 1698, with ornamentation. This was the first movement from *Dido and Aeneas* to be published.

till my grief be known, I Lan——guiſh, till my grief be known, yet wou'd not, yet wou'd not, wou'd not have it gue————ſt.

Peace and I are ſtran-gers grown, Peace and I are ſtran-gers, ſtran—gers grown.

O, O let me Weep! a Two Part SONG.

VIOLIN.

O, O let me, O,

O let me, let me weep!

9. Portrait of Henry Purcell in oil by John Closterman (1656–1713), thought to have been painted after Purcell's death. An engraving of this portrait was printed (in reverse) as a frontispiece to *Orpheus Britannicus*, 1698.

6

Musical and Dramatic Structure

The libretto of 1689 divides the opera into four relatively equal parts—the Prologue, and Acts I, II, and III. Each of the acts, moreover, is divisible into halves: Act I at the entrance of Aeneas, Act II between the Cave scene with the witches and the Grove scene with the court, and Act III between the scene with the sailors and witches and that with Dido and Aeneas and Dido's attendants. Thus, excluding the Prologue, the opera may be seen to contain six scenes, and the musical score illustrates that Purcell identified them by associating each with a separate key area: in order, C minor, C major, F minor-major, D minor-major, B flat major, and G minor.

From Tate's libretto it would appear that these were organized into three groups of two scenes. In the playbook from the 1700 production of *Dido*, the layout of these six scenes is altered so that the third and fourth scenes are reversed. In the Tenbury manuscript the six scenes are back in their original order, but they are apparently organized into two groups of three scenes each; that is, the first three scenes are grouped together as 'Part I', and the fourth scene, which is labelled Act II, and the fifth and sixth scenes, labelled Act III, together make up the 'Second Part', which is not so named. The only consistency in layout among these versions is the use of six distinct scenes both musically and dramatically.

Purcell's use of one key area for each scene, like his use of two distinct dance types, reflects musical traditions of the English masque that stretch back to pre-Commonwealth productions. For example, *The Triumph of Peace* (1633), written by James Shirley and composed by William Lawes, contains a series of nine musically continuous musical scenes, three of which survive. The first is in C major. The opening sinfonia of the second is also in C major, but the texted portions are all in A minor. Similarly, the sinfonia of the third scene is in A minor, but the texted portions

are all in C major. This rather simple procedure was expanded in
Matthew Locke's music for James Shirley's *Cupid and Death*,
which was performed twice during the Commonwealth—in
1653 (perhaps with music by Christopher Gibbons only) and in
1659.[18] Locke's music sets off each of the first four 'entries' or acts
by the use of a single key area; the fifth act contains three. The
succession of keys admits of no harmonic continuity, but rather
vivid sectionalization: G major, A major, F major, D minor, D
major, E minor, and A major.

Closer to Purcell's time is John Blow's *Venus and Adonis*
(c.1685), which consists of a Prologue and three acts. Each has its
own key area, but like Lawes's masque fifty years before, there is
an attempt to bridge the key change by offering a single
movement at the beginning or end of an act in the key of the
adjacent act. The major key areas are C major/G major, A minor,
F major, and G minor.[19] Unlike Locke's keys, these are all quite
closely related (through C major), and it is noteworthy that like
Purcell's opera, Blow's masque begins in C major and ends in G
minor.

Purcell's harmonic organization of *Dido*, therefore, follows
English tradition, and it is up-to-date in the use of related keys
that underscore the dramatic continuity of the action while still
allowing for strong sectionalization in the juxtaposition of different tonal areas. But beyond this, Purcell's harmonic art is
revolutionary in its association of each key with specific emotions
or dramatic situations.

The first scene in C minor would appear to represent Dido's
emotional turmoil or, as she herself calls it, 'grief'.[20] The key, like
the emotion, is uninterrupted, unmitigated. The succession of
movement titles in this section underscores the dominant feeling:
'Shake the cloud from off your brow', 'Banish sorrow, banish
care', 'Ah, Belinda, I am prest', 'Grief increases by concealing',
'When monarchs unite', 'Whence could so much virtue spring'.

---

[18] See Ellen T. Harris, *Handel and the Pastoral Tradition* (London: Oxford University
Press, 1980), 122–5.

[19] See Ibid., 126–9.

[20] The following summary will necessarily need to repeat some of the information
given previously in the synopsis of the plot. Its purpose, however, is to illustrate the
musical layout, giving movement titles, performing forces, forms, and keys. It also serves
to bring into action the conclusions of the preceding sections on literary antecedents of the
libretto and on the manuscript and early printed sources of the opera.

In 'Banish sorrow' the musical setting of the word 'grief'
illustrates its growth, just as Dido's 'languishing' expands in 'Ah,
Belinda'. (See Part III, Chap. 9, Examples 31 and 32.)

In the second scene the key changes to C major, and the mood
shifts to a celebration of the mutual love of Aeneas and Dido.
Belinda and the Second Woman begin this scene with the duet,
'Fear no danger to ensue, the hero loves as well as you'. This sets
the scene for Aeneas's entrance (Belinda: 'See, see your royal guest
appears'), and the first words uttered by the hero proclaim his
undying love for Dido—'Let Dido smile and I'll defy the feeble
stroke of destiny'. The music, however, conveys a different
message, for Aeneas does not sing in C major, the key that
represents their union, but begins in G major and moves quickly
by the end of the movement to E minor. This is the first cadence
of any movement in the opera to a tonic besides C. The following
chorus ('Cupid only throws the dart') refers to Aeneas's situation
and remains in 'his' key of E minor. Afterwards Aeneas resumes
his courtship of Dido ('If not for mine, for empire's sake'),
beginning in E minor and moving to G major. Dido does not
answer, so Belinda hastens to encourage Aeneas in his romantic
quest ('Pursue thy conquest, Love') by emphasizing, as in 'Fear no
danger', the couple's mutual love for one another. The key
returns to C major.

During the following guitar dance, which must also be in C
major, Dido probably gives some sign that she accepts Aeneas's
suit. There follows the concluding chorus about the 'triumphs of
love' ('To the hills and the vales') and The Triumphing Dance.
Both are in C major.

The third scene introduces the Sorceress and her witches; their
key, and that of the scene, is F minor moving to F major. The
action of this scene occurs simultaneously with the royal hunt,
scene iv, which is mentioned and actually intrudes upon this scene
musically and dramatically. At first the Sorceress calls her sister
witches in F minor ('Wayward sisters, you that fright the lonely
traveller by night'), and they enter with a chorus in F major
('Harm's our delight and mischief all our skill'). Then the
Sorceress unveils her plan to destroy the happiness of Dido and
Aeneas. She begins in the tonic minor, telling of 'The Queen of
Carthage', and cadences to the dominant. Her attendants laugh
(also in the dominant: the laughing chorus 'Ho, ho, ho'). Then she

tells of 'The Trojan prince', and completes her plan in the tonic major. The witches again laugh, again echoing her key. Although every movement to this point in the scene is in F major or minor, there already has been one tonal interruption. During the second section of the Sorceress's declamation the hunting horns of the royal chase are heard passing by; that is, the sound of the horns is imitated in the orchestra by the strings. Although these instruments have no tonal limitations that would demand a specific key, the horn call is given in D major, the key of the hunting scene to follow. In fact, the following duet of two witches, which details their plans to ruin the hunt with a storm ('But ere we this perform') is also, like the hunt, in D (minor). The scene closes as the witches move to prepare the 'charm' ('In our deep vaulted cell'), and the music returns to F major. The chorus is followed by the Echo Dance, also in F major.

The royal hunt, scene iv, is in D minor-major. The opening 'Ritornelle', the chorus 'Thanks to these lonesome vales', the guitar dance (by presumption), and the Second Woman's song ('Oft she visits') are all in D minor. The worship and entertainment ended, Aeneas begins to speak proudly about the success of the hunt ('Behold upon my bending spear'); the music is still in D minor. But during the entertainment a dark storm has gathered, and Dido responds not to Aeneas but comments instead on the threatening sky; she urges all to hurry back to court, and the chorus takes up the call ('Haste, haste to town'). The music moves into D major.

When this chorus ends, only Aeneas and perhaps two of his closest attendants remain on stage. (At this point in the 1700 version two of Aeneas's friends are given dialogue to speak; although speechless in 1689, they may well have been present nevertheless.) As the three turn to follow Dido and her court, the Spirit enters ('Stay, Prince, and hear great Jove's command'). At first incredulous, Aeneas then accepts his fate and orders his ships to weigh anchor that very night. The Spirit vanishes, and Aeneas's attendants most probably rush out to tell the crew. Aeneas, however, stays behind and muses on his decision, its effects on Dido, and ultimately on his own feelings.

According to the musical manuscripts, Aeneas's soliloquy ends this scene (see Plate 4). The entire section beginning with the Spirit's entrance, however, has been in A minor, not in the key of the scene as a whole. The situation seems harmonically to reflect back to Aeneas's entrance in Act I, which had also occurred outside the main key of the scene. Undoubtedly in both cases Aeneas is meant to be seen as a disruptive force, but still one might think that the scene should end in the proper key. As the 1689 libretto indicates a chorus and dance for the witches after Aeneas's exit (see Plate 3), it is possible that these movements, now lost, originally served this purpose. The problem of this scene, however, will need to be discussed in more detail below.

The fifth scene illustrates the preparations of the sailors for departure, while the witches stand by and revel in their success. All of the movements are in B flat major; there is no tonal interruption, no hesitation in the action. Again, as in the first scene, the succession of movement titles helps to indicate the directness of the action: 'Come away, fellow sailors', 'The Sailors Dance', 'See the flags and streamers curling', 'Our next motion must be to storm her lover on the ocean', 'Destruction's our delight', and 'Jack of Lanthorn Dance'.

The last scene, depicting Dido's death, is in G minor. Again in this scene there is no tonal interruption, no turning back from Dido's fate. First Dido and Aeneas confront one another ('Your counsel all is urged in vain'); Dido orders him away. At Aeneas's exit there is a clear G minor cadence. Dido then sings a single couplet of text: 'But death, alas! I cannot shun; Death must come when he is gone.' This ends on a half cadence. The chorus follows with, 'Great minds against themselves conspire', which cadences to the tonic G minor. Dido then sings her great lament, 'Thy hand, Belinda'—'When I am laid in earth'. Like the earlier statement Dido makes about death, the first part of this air (in which Dido sings that 'death invades' her) ends on a half cadence. The second part of the air cadences, of course, to G minor; the cadence coincides with Dido's death. The final chorus ('With drooping wings ye Cupids come') and its repetition, which may represent the Cupids Dance, are in G minor as well.

Purcell's sense of tonality in *Dido* is thus particularly secure. Within the traditional framework of the English masque, he has composed each of the six sections in a single key. But these are not unrelated, as Locke's had been, and furthermore, each key clearly represents a specific action. Scenes i, v, and vi are tonally stable: scene i and C minor represent Dido's 'grief' or torment; scene v and B flat major represent the Sorceress's success; scene vi and G minor represent Dido's death. The tonal security is even more evident, however, in the scenes containing harmonic interruptions. The most obvious example occurs in the third scene in F minor-major, where the sections in D major-minor clearly refer to the hunt and the tonality of the hunting scene. Just as the noise of the hunt interrupts the plotting to bring about Dido's downfall, the key of D major-minor interrupts the key of the scene.

Purcell's use of tonality also offers a clear indication of how Aeneas's role should be interpreted. In his first two appearances, his music is interruptive of the tonality of the scene. In scene ii, Aeneas's entrance disturbs the C major tonality with a shift to E minor. The following chorus about Aeneas, 'Cupid only throws the dart', confirms the E minor tonality. Purcell thus depicts the disruption that has been caused by Aeneas's arrival in Carthage as well as the disturbance that has occurred in everyone's emotions. Only after the newcomer concludes speaking, and Belinda resumes her encouragement of the match between Aeneas and Dido, does the music return to C major. The fourth scene is obviously more problematic since there is no tonal return. Still, Aeneas's music is disruptive of the key of the scene. The dialogue with the Spirit and Aeneas's concluding monologue occur in A minor rather than D minor-major. Throughout the opera, then, Aeneas's music is centred on A and E minor, whereas Dido's music is centred on C and G minor. Dido's music is always 'in tune' with the scene; Aeneas's is not. The striking contrast in the harmonic handling of these two characters seems too remarkable to be coincidental.

Purcell's use of harmonic identification can be compared to Blow's harmonic usage in *Venus and Adonis*. Act I of this opera is set in A minor, and this key is initially used to depict the love between the goddess and young hunter. Hunting music from offstage interrupts the idyll and interrupts the key of the section as well by being in C major. When the hunters enter, however, the music immediately returns to A minor. There is no dramatic continuity between these two vocal sections that Blow sets in the same key, but there is direct continuity between the hunting music and the scene with the hunters, which Blow sets in different keys. At the end of the act when the hunting music returns, it is again in C major, but this tonal allusion to the hunt, and undoubtedly to hunting horns, never carries over, as does Purcell's, to the hunters themselves, who in Blow's masque remain tonally undifferentiated from the lovers whom they have interrupted.

Purcell's careful planning of tonal areas thus contrasts sharply with Blow's less dramatically organized layout, and knowing this should help us to solve the apparent problems at the end of the fourth scene. Except in this case, all of Purcell's tonally-defined sections are closed harmonically. Furthermore, following the layout given by the 1689 libretto, the two scenes of each act form a major-minor pair, using either the parallel or relative minor. Thus the first act moves from C minor to C major; the last act moves from B flat major to G minor; and the second act should possibly move from the F major ending of the witches' scene to a D minor ending of the hunting scene. Acknowledging the primacy of the 1689 libretto and the apparently logical harmonic layout of the acts within that pattern will lead necessarily to the conclusion that, in fact, something is missing from the end of scene iv.

Eric Walter White has hypothesized that the two movements at the end of Tate's Act II were lost as a result of the alterations made in the score for the 1700 production.[21] In this version, the scenes of the second act were reversed. Although this change results in dramatic chaos, for Aeneas meets the false Mercury before the Sorceress conjures up the apparition, it allows for a spectacular ending to the act. The Grove (or hunting) scene was then altered, not to address the dramatic anomaly caused by the scene reversal, but to expand Aeneas's response to the Spirit. Thus immediately after his monologue, which in the musical sources ends the act, new text was added so that Aeneas could discuss his course of action with two friends; they argue whether he should obey love or honour. After this insertion, the text for the witches' chorus is given just as it had appeared in the 1689 libretto.

White argues that the differences between the 1689 libretto and the musical sources result from copying errors made after the 1700 performance. He surmises that a scribe told to reorder the scenes did so correctly but grouped them so that the witches' scene still ended an act and the hunting scene still began one; thus

---

[21] See E. W. White, 'New Light'.

creating an Act I with three scenes and an Act II with only one. Further, when told to drop the added material after Aeneas's monologue, the scribe inadvertently dropped Purcell's original ending to the act as well. White then suggests that the surviving musical version represents that performed in 1704, which conclusion can be confirmed with the additional reasons given above.

White's argument appears quite plausible up to a point, but it fails to ask why the person requesting this score would not have noticed such glaring errors, especially if it was to be used in performance. Furthermore, the two-part division in the Tenbury manuscript, although not corroborated by the previous librettos, makes a good deal of musical sense, and the evidence of the music cannot be so easily dismissed. I have shown elsewhere that the two parts of the Tenbury score are musically symmetrical in the succession of movements and in key structure.[22] In addition to this, however, the movements that are paired musically are typically contrasted dramatically to illustrate the conflicts of the plot (Table 1).

Scenes i and iv both begin with independent instrumental movements, the only scenes in the opera to do so. Both scenes then continue with a song by Belinda that sets the general mood after which the chorus repeats the sentiment. In scene iv, the exact repetition by the chorus may, as discussed above, be an addition of Purcell's. The next song in both scenes is written over a ground bass, the first telling of Dido's torment, the latter contrasting this with the tale of Actaeon's fate. A similar contrast occurs in the final choruses, where that in scene i tells of how delightful it is for monarchs to unite, and that in scene iv ('Haste, haste') pin-points the moment at which Dido and Aeneas are separated. Once again, the chorus in scene iv may have been Purcell's addition. The scenes both close with declamation, pairing Dido's hesitation to trust her feelings with Aeneas's decision to forsake the Queen.

In the second pair of scenes the conflict is even more in evidence. Both begin with solos that are repeated by the chorus. In scene ii Belinda and the Second Woman sing 'Fear no danger to ensue, / The hero loves as well as you', whereas in scene v the sailor and his friends sing of leaving their shore molls with 'vows of returning / Though never intending to visit them more'. In

---

[22] See Harris, *Handel and the Pastoral Tradition*, 133-6.

TABLE 1: *Formal Symmetries in* Dido and Aeneas

Scene	
1	symphony—song—chorus—song—declamation—song— chorus—declamation
4	ritornello—song— →chorus—song—declamation—song— → chorus—declamation
2	song— →chorus—declamation—chorus—declamation— song—chorus—dance
5	song— →chorus —dance—declamation— song—chorus—dance

3	declamation—chorus— $\begin{Bmatrix} \text{declamation} \\ \text{chorus} \end{Bmatrix}$ —song—chorus— dance
6	declamation—chorus— $\begin{Bmatrix} \text{declamation} \\ \text{song} \end{Bmatrix}$ — —chorus— [dance]

THE SCENES

1	Dido and her attendants	4	the hunting scene
2	Aeneas's entrance	5	the sailors' departure
3	the witches' plotting	6	Dido's death

— → indicates that the following chorus is a repetition of the preceding song.

scene v, the choral repetition was added by Purcell. In the declamatory passages that follow, Aeneas, in scene ii, sings of himself, 'Make not in a hopeless fire / A hero fall and Troy once more expire'; but the true situation reveals itself in the parallel movement, in scene v, where the witches sing of Dido, 'Our plot has took, / The Queen's forsook, Eliza's ruin'ed'.

The chorus in scene ii telling of Aeneas's 'love wound' has no textual companion in scene v, but it can be paired with the Sailors Dance—the only independent dance movement of the opera that does not come at the end of a scene. The instructions in the 1689 libretto do not demand an independent dance at this point, for the sailors could easily have danced to the previous chorus, 'Come away, fellow sailors'. That Purcell used a separate movement

seems to indicate a perceived need for an additional musical
number at this point to achieve the desired balance. At any rate,
these two scenes continue in perfect symmetry. Belinda's song
urging Aeneas to 'pursue thy conquest', is paired with the
Sorceress's song revealing that Aeneas will be pursued with
storms at sea. And finally, the court sings of the 'Triumphs of
Love and of Beauty', whereas the witches revel in the triumph of
their schemes for destruction ('Destruction's our delight'). Both
scenes end with independent dance movements.

The last pair of scenes presents the culmination of the dramatic
situation in each part. Scene iii begins with the introduction of the
Sorceress and her evil plan; scene vi with the final confrontation
between Dido and Aeneas. In the former this climaxes in a large
section of declamation with choral interruptions, the entire group
accompanied by strings ('The Queen of Carthage'). At this point
in the last section Dido sings of her ultimate fate in declamation
and song, and the song is also accompanied by strings ('When I
am laid in earth'). These are the only vocal pieces in the opera
with independent string accompaniment, and the use of such
accompaniment in these two solos helps to emphasize the characters of the Sorceress and Dido whose conflict wholly underlies
and motivates the action of the drama. Aeneas is merely a pawn.
At the ends of these two scenes the results of the conflict are
summarized; the witches retire to their 'deep-vaulted cell', Dido
to a rose-scattered tomb.

Throughout the opera, then, the movements are musically
paired while they tend to be textually opposed, revealing the
central conflicts of the drama—between good and evil, chastity
and licence. The musical symmetries are only possible, however,
because of (1) the addition of an independent instrumental
introduction to scene iv balancing the introduction to scene i, (2)
the addition of an independent dance movement in the middle of
scene v (the only one), (3) the addition of a number of choruses
not indicated in the libretto, and (4) the omission of the chorus
and dance at the end of scene iv. However, it is still not possible to
say whether the symmetries revealed by this analysis were part of
the original performance. Nevertheless, many of the obvious
obstacles to the acceptance of such an argument can be overcome.

First of all, the two-part division of the opera appears to
conflict with the use of time in the libretto, where the first two

scenes occur at the same time (probably in the evening of the first day), the second two scenes occur simultaneously (in the morning of the second day), and the last two scenes occur continuously (in the late afternoon of the second day). Thus the grouping of scenes two plus two plus two makes better 'temporal' sense than three plus three. Dramatically, however, the break between scene iii and iv represents the exact middle of the opera. Before this point Dido has succumbed to her emotions, and the witches have conceived their evil plan. In the remainder of the opera these actions find their resolution. First Aeneas meets the Spirit and agrees to leave. Then he departs from Dido and Carthage, and finally Dido dies. The use of the Ritornelle at this point also helps to divide the opera between action and reaction.

Second, the two-part division conflicts with the tonal structure of the opera if each pair of two scenes is seen as a major-minor pair, as discussed above. However, each of the second-act scenes moves from major to minor independently. In fact, the 1689 libretto gives only four scenic divisions, and these relate to the harmony as follows: Act I (the Palace) scenes i and ii—C minor to major; Act II (the Cave) scene iii—F minor to major, (the Grove) scene iv—D minor to major; and Act III (the Ships) scenes v and vi—B flat major to G minor. Thus, the two-part division can be understood to divide the opera scenically and harmonically into halves without any disruption of the overall tonal plan of successive major-minor pairs. Furthermore, each set of three sections moves symmetrically from the minor to major dominant to the tonic, in the first case through the parallel minor tonic and in the second through the relative major of the tonic. Finally, in the two-part division the ending of the fourth scene in the 'wrong key' does not occur at the conclusion of a major section of the opera, and if a rounded harmonic form is strongly desired for this scene, it can be achieved by simply repeating the scene's opening D minor Ritornelle—a use for this movement that may even be suggested by its name.[23]

Third, the three-part division is indicated not only in the 1689 libretto, but it is maintained in the 1700 playbook, and even the Tenbury manuscript refers to three acts. It has been shown, however, that the 1700 playbook often perpetuates errors from

---

[23] I am grateful to Robin Langley for suggesting this use of the Ritornelle.

the earlier libretto, and since the use of the opera within the play demanded four separate entertainments (including the Prologue), the scenes may have been differently divided just as they were differently ordered.

Fourth, the problematic ending of the fourth scene cannot be easily dismissed. Not only is it clear from the 1689 libretto that it was Tate's original plan to include a chorus and dance for the witches at the end of this scene, but the text for the chorus and indication for the dance still appear in the 1700 playbook. Furthermore, at the parallel passage in Tate's *Brutus of Alba* (Act IV), the witches end the scene. This, however, is the only time in the play that the witches gloat over their success, whereas in the much shorter opera, if they retain the ending to scene iv, the witches enter twice in succession to revel in their triumphs—once after Aeneas speaks to the Spirit and again (in scene v) after the sailors make ready for their departure. Thus they would conclude two consecutive scenes in a very similar way.[24] Perhaps this was seen as a fault and the earlier text excised.

Fifth, and finally, the two-part division conflicts with the apparent musical continuity found in the Tenbury manuscript between scenes iii and iv. That is, the final bar of the Echo Dance and the upbeat to the following Ritornelle are rhythmically related as shown in Figure 1. The metres of both pieces are the same (common time) and the rhythmical values given in the partial bars that end and begin these consecutive movements combine to make one complete bar. If this notation derives from the original score, then it offers musical evidence that Purcell conceived the third and fourth scenes as a musical unit.

FIGURE I

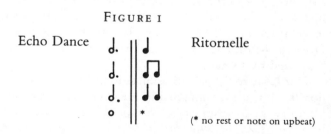

(* no rest or note on upbeat)

[24] And this would mean that the witches actually end three scenes in a row—the Cave, the Grove, and the Ships.

No one of the five points discussed above can in itself override the implications for a two-part division as found in the music itself. Taken together, however, they create a strong argument for the three-part division. Although it may never be possible to determine exactly the relationship between the structure given in the Tenbury manuscript and the original performance of *Dido*, it is clear that the score does not represent an exact copy of the 1689 version. To summarize, there are certain aspects of the Tenbury manuscript that definitely seem to result from the revisions made for the 1704 performance—in particular, the expansion of Belinda's part at the expense of both the Second Woman and Dido. On the other hand, the Tenbury manuscript seems to offer the only correct reading in other respects—as in a number of cases concerning the assignment of lines to the Sorceress and her witches. And finally, the Tenbury manuscript sometimes preserves changes that were presumably made in 1700—for example, the alteration of fairies into furies, and the Jack of Lanthorn pantomime to The Witches Dance.

Although the Tenbury manuscript maintains elements from all three of the earliest productions of *Dido* in 1689, 1700, and 1704, a comparison of these sources indicates that it most likely derives from the 1704 performances. This comparison, however, also indicates that the surviving music for *Dido and Aeneas* must correspond closely to Purcell's original score.

7

Musical Declamation

It has already been shown that *Dido* depends on aspects of the English masque tradition for its overall harmonic structure and for its use of two distinct types of dances. The same may be said for other elements of its musical style as well—in particular the use of musical declamation. The antecedents of this style stretch back to the beginning of the century, and by studying them it will be possible to gain a better understanding of Purcell's own remarkable achievement.

At the turn of the seventeenth century, when Italian musical culture was immersed in the development of a successful musical recitative, England witnessed the greatest period of spoken drama in its history. Its strength derived not only from Shakespeare, but also from Marlowe, Beaumont, Fletcher, Jonson and others. The impact of the works produced by these playwrights was such that England remained hesitant throughout the seventeenth century to give up the spoken word. Even after the French capitulated to the operas of Lully, and after public opera houses opened in Germany (Hamburg, 1678), England resisted. The period of the Restoration (1660–98) saw the works of Shakespeare and Fletcher, among others, revised and fitted out with increasingly elaborate musical sections, but the play still did not give in to musically continuous opera. Only with the importation of foreign composers did England succumb to opera of this type, and then almost exclusively to Italian opera in Italian. The serious efforts to establish all-sung English opera in the 1710s and 1730s did not succeed in overthrowing the Italian opera, but the ballad opera, where the musical elements were once again inserted into a spoken play, became highly popular beginning in the 1720s. Neither the trend towards Italian opera nor that for ballad opera, however, demanded the development of an English declamatory or recitative style; still, the style was cultivated.

As early as 1617 the English composer Nicholas Lanier

(1588–1666) may have imitated Italian recitative in his music for two masques by Ben Jonson. At least the 1640 publications of *Lovers Made Men* and *The Vision of Delight* so indicate, where in the former it is stated explicitly that 'the whole Masque was sung after the Italian manner, *stilo recitativo*'. The one surviving fragment of music, however, does not support this claim.[25]

Nevertheless, recitative, or that type of music that allows a text to be declaimed according to speech rhythms in a natural, ongoing fashion and without formal structures and repetitions, quite clearly fascinated Lanier. He travelled to Italy, studied the compositional techniques developed there, and on his return composed a long monologue in recitative style, *Hero's Complaint to Leander*, which was modelled after similar Italian laments.[26] The unusualness (and success) of this composition may be demonstrated by its publication by John Playford in a volume of songs in 1683, some fifty years after its composition; during the intervening period, no example of English declamation had superseded Lanier's efforts.

At least two composers, however, did follow in Lanier's footsteps—the brothers William and Henry Lawes. Henry (1596–1662) composed a recitative scene that became almost as renowned as Lanier's. *Ariadne deserted by Theseus*, like *Hero's Complaint to Leander*, is a solo lament to be sung by a woman; Playford published it in 1653. Henry also collaborated with John Milton for two masques performed privately: *Arcades* (1633) and *Comus* (1634). But in these the spoken word still reigned supreme; the extant score for *Comus*, which has the more music of the two, contains but five songs.

The work of William Lawes (1602–45) illustrates a stronger interest in musically continuous settings. Some of his masques include long stretches of text all to be sung—masques such as *The*

---

[25] See Harris, 'Recitative and Aria in *Dido and Aeneas*', in *Studies in the History of Music*, ii (1987) for a more complete discussion of the use of the term *stilo recitativo* in seventeenth-century England. The surviving musical fragment from *Lovers Made Men* is printed and discussed in McDonald Emslie, 'Nicholas Lanier's Innovations in English Song', *Music and Letters*, xli (1960), 25; Andrew Sabol, *Four Hundred Songs and Dances from the Stuart Masque*, 87–8; and Ian Spink, *English Song: Dowland to Purcell* (London, 1974), 47–8.

[26] The most popular lament and the most probable model for Lanier was the lament from Monteverdi's *Arianna*. Nino Pirrotta, in *Music and Theatre from Poliziano to Monteverdi*, by Pirrotta and Elena Povoledo (Cambridge: Cambridge University Press, 1975), 276, writes, 'After *Arianna* [1608] composers became so conscious of the effectiveness of the lament that they abused it to the point of caricature.'

Triumph of Peace and *Britannia Triumphans*. At least one, *The Triumphs of the Prince d'Amour*, seems certainly to have been sung throughout, although not all of its music survives.[27] William Lawes's masques, however, represent the first important musical precedent to Purcell's *Dido and Aeneas*; therefore, it will be valuable to look closely at one that contains an abundant amount of extant music.

The Triumph of Peace was written by James Shirley and first performed on 3 February 1633. It begins with the arrival of Opinion, Confidence, Novelty, and Admiration, who discuss the imminently expected arrival of Fancy at court. Fancy enters with Jollity and Laughter and is asked to prepare antimasques, or danced entertainments. These were meant to precede the entry of the proper masquers and were usually comic in nature, episodic, and largely unrelated to the masque that followed.[28] In *The Triumph of Peace* the five antimasques consist, not unusually, of spoken dialogue interspersed with pantomimed dances; that is, there is no singing. After the fifth and last dance, one of the antimasque characters hears other music—'What new change is this? these strains are heavenly'. This not-so-subtle device marks the beginning of the masque proper; the antimasquers 'go off fearfully'.

The masque itself is made up dramatically of a series of nine 'songs', each of which comprises an entire musical section. The first introduces and is sung by Irene (Peace). In the second Irene calls up her sisters, Eunonia, representing the Law, and Diche, representing Justice, who appear in the third and fourth sections respectively. The fifth song ends this section with a choral invocation to the King and Queen.

The masquers, sixteen sons of Peace, Law, and Justice, then appear and are invited to dance in a speech made by Genius. After they 'dance their entry to the violins', the chorus sings a second ode in honour of the royal couple. The 'Masquers dance their main dance', after which 'a Carpenter, a Painter, one of the Black

---

[27] The complete texts and extant music for these three masques have been published along with extensive commentaries by Murray Lefkowitz, *Trois Masques à la Cour de Charles Ier d'Angleterre* (Paris: Éditions du Centre National de la Recherche Scientifique, 1970).

[28] For more information on the term antimasque and the role of Ben Jonson in its development, see Enid Welsford, *The Court Masque: A Study in the Relationship between Poetry and the Revels* (New York: Russell and Russell, Inc., 1962).

guard, a Tailor, the Tailor's Wife, an Embroiderer's Wife, a feather-maker's Wife, and a Property Man's Wife' interrupt the scene with rough talk and a dance. The Tailor ends this episode with the comment, 'Now let us go off cleanly, and somebody will think this was meant for an antimasque'.

The proper masquers are then encouraged in Song VII to dance with the ladies in the audience (Revels). This being done, Amphiluche (forerunner of morning) calls the masquers to retire and, as they go, to bless the King and Queen (Songs VIII and IX). The masque ends with a spoken Epilogue to their royal Majesties.

This long description has served to lay out a typical Caroline masque that begins with a series of comic pantomimed dances (antimasques) weakly strung together with spoken dialogue. The masque proper is also dance-oriented in its presentation of the masquers and their entry dance, main dance, revels, and exit dance. The dances of this section, however, are not connected by means of spoken dialogue but, for the most part, by means of a continuous musical setting that helps to emphasize the heightened plane. Appropriately, the single comic interruption returns to speech.

The setting for the musically continuous first three 'songs' survives; its harmonic plan has been discussed above. Song I begins with a 'Simfony' followed by Irene's 'song', 'Hence ye profane'. The chorus concludes the section by repeating the first line of Irene's song as a refrain but with a different setting. All of Song I is in C major.

Song II also begins with a 'Simfony'. Then Irene calls to her sisters ('Wherefore do my sisters stay?') and is answered by a trio ('See where she shines—In her celestiall gayety'). The symphony is in C major but the vocal sections move into A minor.

Song III begins with a 'Simfony' in A minor; it continues with a dialogue for Eunonia and Irene—that is, a song that begins with alternation of the voices and concludes with a short duet. It and the final chorus are both in C major.

The most striking aspect of this musical sequence is that there is no recitative. The continuous setting consists rather of a linked series of short and well-defined instrumental pieces, songs, and choruses. The songs emphasize declamation, yet are songs still. Take, for example, the first song in *The Triumph of Peace*, 'Hence, ye profane' (Example 2).

Example 2: 'Hence, ye profane' from *The Triumph of Peace* by
    William Lawes, as edited by Murray Lefkowitz in
    Trois Masques à la Cour de Charles Ier d'Angleterre
    (Paris: Éditions du Centre National de la Recherche
    Scientifiques, 1970)

The music unfolds within a strict metrical framework yet with
no rhythmic patterning. That is, although each bar differs
rhythmically from the next, the underlying beat remains regular
and strong. The rhythmic inflections of the individual words can
then be gauged against this beat. Thus 'starry' is carefully set
within the first half of a bar as ♪♩., whereas 'glorious' and 'aged'
are given as ♩.♪ . All three words are accented on the first
syllable, and in each the accented syllable falls properly on the
strong beat. Beyond this, however, Lawes has also underscored
the differing rhythmic values of the words themselves. The
stressed syllable can be long or short, and the correctness of
Lawes's settings can be easily perceived by attempting to reverse
the rhythmic pattern of 'starry' (to ♩.♪) and 'aged' (to ♪♩.).
The first loses its twinkle; the latter becomes very ungrateful to
sing.[29]

[29] I am very grateful to Katherine Rohrer for carefully reading this section and offering
many insights into the analysis of word rhythm and declamation. For more detailed studies
of English word rhythm see David Abercrombie, 'Syllable Quantity and Enclitics', in *In
Honour of David Jones*, ed. Abercrombie (London, 1964), 216–22; and Katherine Rohrer,
'The Energy of English Words' (Unpublished Ph.D. dissertation: Princeton University,
1980).

Similar care is also taken over longer words, and the setting of 'another' ([♪]♩♪♩.) can be contrasted with 'created' ([♪]♩♪♩). In both cases not only is the accented syllable placed on an accented (second) beat, but the duration of each syllable is carefully planned to suit the word. Neither setting would fit the other word as well despite the similarity of syllable count and accent.

Lawes also gives close attention to phrase structure and meaning. The opening line ordering 'Fancy and the rest' away is sung to an arpeggiated C major chord that resembles a trumpet call. The second line is harmonically framed by a move into the dominant (G major). This harmony is maintained for the third phrase; the fourth returns to C major. The fifth phrase moves into the relative minor (A), and the last modulates back to the tonic.

The words of the second phrase are highlighted by an elision of the second accented beat in the second bar. This ensures a displaced accent on the word 'you' and the syncopation illustrates not only how 'sick' time has become but how out of place (literally and figuratively) the 'you' (antimasque characters) are. In the third phrase the little run on 'delight'—the only word not set syllabically—ornaments its meaning. Perhaps, however, the most striking aspect of the careful composition is the rising line of the successive phrases. 'Time hath sick feathers' begins on c"; 'delight' takes the line up to d", and the first 'starry' sky is still higher on e". But the second and 'new' sky created by the light from the eyes of the King and Queen is not only 'brighter' but higher—the f" on 'new' takes the phrase appropriately to the highest note of the song.

This kind of careful declamatory song-writing (with control over the melodic and harmonic as well as rhythmic elements) derives from the earliest years of the seventeenth century in England,[30] when it was clearly contrasted with the dance song, which was often in triple metre and frequently contained repetitive rhythmic patterns. Less care was taken in the dance song with the word accents and meaning, and, in many, successive stanzas were repeated to the same tune. One example by Henry Lawes will suffice to show the extreme differences between these styles that remained a part of English style throughout the seventeenth century (Example 3).

[30] For a more historical approach to the declamatory air and other seventeenth-century song types, see Spink, *English Song*, and Harris, 'Recitative and Aria'.

Example 3: 'Love's Scrutiny' by Henry Lawes, taken from *The Treasury of Musick*, published by John Playford, 1669

(three more stanzas following to the same music)

Note the pattern of three repeated minums with which the song begins. Later this is picked up to begin a sequence in bar 8. The break from this sequence is then made only melodically; the rhythm still persists and leads into the cadence. Such repetitive rhythmic patterning, often complimented in the second half of the century by a repetitive ground bass, typified the dance air.

The declamatory air, therefore, was deemed more suitable for dramatic situations as the music was more subordinated to the words. This style was often found in songs composed for Elizabethan and Jacobean as well as Caroline dramas; it is no surprise that it was taken over into the masque. In many ways the declamatory air of the first half of the seventeenth century substituted in England for continental recitative. However, it never became highly emotional or affective; in intervals and harmony it remained largely triadic and often static. Its purpose mainly was to heighten the words, not reflect the meaning.

The development of a more flexible (or continental) recitative style in England was prevented, at least in part, by the use of regularly rhymed lyrics (such as are still found in Tate's libretto). Thus the period of the Interregnum (1642–60) saw repeated attempts to create a more appropriate text for recitative. In 1650 William Davenant discussed a new verse form—ABAB—that might allow more flexibility for recitative than the rhymed couplet. In 1654 Richard Flecknoe wrote of his hope of introducing recitative to England. And in 1656 Davenant actually produced an 'opera', *The Siege of Rhodes*, with its five acts ('entries') composed by Henry Lawes, Captain Cooke, and Matthew Locke.

Davenant states that the music was in recitative style, and, in fact, in 1662 John Evelyn commented enthusiastically about the 'recitative musick' in *The Siege of Rhodes*. In 1670 Dryden wrote that *The Siege* was first 'performed in recitative music' and later revived as a 'just drama'.[31] The music apparently is lost, but there is no reason to assume that these Englishmen meant anything different by the term 'recitative musick' than is clearly implied in the Jonson–Lanier collaboration (based on scansion of the text and the one extant piece of music) or found in the masque *The Triumphs of the Prince d'Amour* (1636) by William Davenant himself and set by William Lawes. The music we know from before *The Siege* clearly points to such a conclusion; the music composed afterwards does so as well.

The three most important composers following the Restoration of the Monarchy in 1660 were Matthew Locke, John Blow, and Henry Purcell. The most important dramatic works of this period issue from their pens. Matthew Locke's music for the 1659 production of James Shirley's *Cupid and Death* closely follows *The Siege of Rhodes* in time and reveals the changes in style that had followed Lawes's setting of Shirley's *The Triumph of Peace*.

Locke, like Lawes, organizes the music of each of the five entries around single keys (the fifth entry has three key areas), and each section is made up of instrumental pieces, solos, and choruses. There is declamation followed by a choral repetition of text in a different setting—'Though little be the God of Love'; there are dialogues—'Apollo once the Python slew'; and there are airs with exact musical repetition by chorus—'Victorious men on Earth'. The masque also contains long stretches of declamation that rival in length the earlier monologues of Lanier and Henry Lawes. Locke's declamatory style, however, leans away from the speech-like accents of his immediate predecessors towards a more lyrical and embellished setting. It is as if Locke felt that the purely musical side of the word-tone relationship needed strengthening.

---

[31] Davenant discussed verse forms in the Preface to his heroic poem, *Gondibert* (1650), which was never set to music. Flecknoe's discussion of recitative may be found in the Preface to his libretto, *Ariadne deserted by Theseus*, which also was never set to music; his comments are reprinted in Haun, *But Hark!* The entry in John Evelyn's diary about Davenant's recitative is dated 9 January 1662. And Dryden's comments on *The Siege of Rhodes* come from his Preface to *The Conquest of Granada* (1672), also known as a self-standing essay entitled 'Of Heroic Plays.'

Particularly noticeable among his stylistic mannerisms are elaborate embellishments on wholly unimportant words. Presumably they are placed in this way to avoid any obstruction in the communication of the text—a bow to declamation—but as they bear no relation to the meaning of the words they carry, they often seem unnecessary decorations of an otherwise plain structure. Sometimes, however, the ornament is simply displaced as shown in Example 4.

In Example 4a, for instance, the run on 'a' seems clearly meant to depict the act of 'wounding'. Similarly the turn figure on 'with' in Example 4b must represent 'shake', and the spinning demisemiquavers in 4c depict 'flame' not 'a'. Surely the meandering run in Example 4d represents 'dream'. Finally, there can be no question that the semiquaver pattern on 'but' in 4e pictures the 'bleeding'; the pain is even expressed in the drop of a diminished

Example 4: Excerpts from *Cupid and Death* by Matthew Locke, as edited by Edward J. Dent (London, 1965), *Musica Britannica*, II

fifth at the beginning of the second group of semiquavers. Such
examples could be multiplied many-fold. Sometimes, but only
rarely, the ornamental passage is integrated with the meaning of
the text. One example will suffice (Example 5).

Example 5: Excerpt from *Cupid and Death* by Matthew Locke

As Locke's declamation moves towards lyricism and song by
means of such embellishments, it turns away from the careful
speech rhythms of Lanier and the Lawes brothers. His style is not
wholly new, however, but reminiscent of declamatory songs
from earlier in the century. One can compare, for example, an
excerpt from a song by Robert Johnson written about 1614
(Example 6).

Looking at the music of Johnson, Lanier, Lawes, and Locke
chronologically, it would appear that Lanier and the Lawes
brothers were moving towards the creation of a native recitative
style. Perhaps without the political interruption of the Commonwealth, this musical development would have continued. As it
happened, however, the Restoration brought with it an increased
interest in the tuneful song, possibly affected by the dance-
influenced French air, and, as a result, the declamatory air, too,
reverted to a more tuneful form. Just as Restoration theatre
returned to plays of Shakespeare and Fletcher, Restoration composers such as Locke seem to have returned to the model of the

Example 6: 'Care-charming sleep', excerpt, by Robert Johnson,
            taken from *The English Lute-Songs*, 2nd Series, vol.
            17, ed. Ian Spink (Composed *c.*1614)

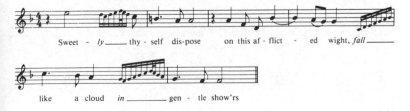

declamatory song by Johnson and his contemporaries. The influence of the intervening years was felt in continued efforts to convey the text clearly, but this resulted in oddities, such as the placement of ornamental passages on totally unimportant words. The emotive content of Locke's songs thus remains quite low despite the use of strongly affective language, and the attention to individual word accent is reduced from before. Despite the obvious difficulties, however, Locke's style of heightened and embellished declamation became more favoured than the more text-oriented style of Lanier and Lawes. The stylistic problems inherent in this declamatory style were effectively worked out in the music of John Blow.

Blow's *Venus and Adonis* (written about 1682–5) is the most important predecessor to Purcell's *Dido and Aeneas*. In the last act Venus sings as she waits longingly for Adonis to return from the hunt (Example 7). The opening repetitions of Adonis's name, ever rising higher, bespeak her anguish. Her following 'sigh' takes the appropriate form of a rising appoggiatura. The vocal line then drops to its lowest point (perhaps describing her bosom as the seat of her emotions) and rises, like her sighs, over the next set of phrases to a' ('rise'), c♯" ('grief'), d" ('dominion'), e" ('eyes'), and f" (mourning). This brings the line back up to the high note achieved during the invocation to Adonis. After an intermediate line telling of 'Tombs and Urns and ev'ry mournful thing' with a

Example 7: *Venus and Adonis*, beginning of third act, by John Blow, as edited by Anthony Lewis (Paris, 1939)

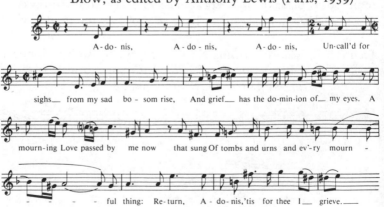

A-do-nis,   A-do-nis,   A-do-nis,   Un-call'd for

sighs__ from my sad   bo-som rise,   And grief__ has the do-min-ion of__ my eyes. A

mourn-ing Love passed by   me now   that sung Of tombs and urns and ev'-ry mourn -

- - - ful thing: Re-turn, A-do-nis,'tis for thee I__ grieve.__

beautiful melisma on 'mournful,' the line finally reaches its highest point on a repeated g″—shared by the words 'thee' and 'I'—the couple joined at the climax of the air.

Throughout the song Blow's short phrases are often infused with meaning; his favourite method is melodic chromaticism. Note the rise by semitones on 'grief', the halting chromatic ascent on a hesitant dotted note figure telling of 'tombs and urns', and the diminished fourth in the setting of 'mournful'. With such melodic details, always appropriate to the text, Blow adds greatly to the emotional content of his declamation.

The general outline of his song—its rising line and meaningful climax—resembles Lawes's 'Hence, ye profane'. Yet the dramatic intensity has increased greatly due to the emotionalism of the words, their context within the drama, and their appropriate musical setting. Blow thus integrates Lawes's phrase structure and Locke's florid declamation into a meaningful framework that aptly portrays deeply-felt and personal emotion. Like Locke, however, Blow does not pay strict attention to individual word accents. Note, for example 'bosom' (♩.♪) and 'dominion' (♪|♪♪); in both cases the accented syllable rightly receives stress through pitch and metric accent (tonic and agogic accent), but the duration of this syllable should be shortened to allow the final syllable its proper breadth: 'bosom' (♪♩.) and 'dominion' (♪|♪♩.). Such shortcomings are minor, however, within the context of Blow's achievement of an emotionally effective declamation. Moreover, only a few years later, Purcell, who was a student of Blow's, would pick up on his teacher's accomplishments and add the concern for individual word accent missing since the time of Lawes. This culmination of traits is apparent in the first long stretch of declamation in *Dido*, 'Whence could so much virtue spring?'(Example 8.)

With Purcell the placing of a short note on the down beat followed by a longer note (♪♩.), the so-called 'Scotch snap', returns as an important method of setting English appropriately—not only on single words, such as 'stubborn' and 'pity' but over two monosyllabic words, such as 'so much' or 'did he'. Purcell's use of this rhythm for 'full of' is not as literally correct, but it highlights the following word ('woe') by separating it from its normal word group. Thus the 'tale' is not '*full* / of woe', but 'full of / *woe*'.

Example 8: 'Whence could so much virtue spring' (as edited by the author)

Example 8: *continued*

Purcell usually reserves the opposite rhythmical set-
ting ($\flat$. $\flat$) for situations that call especially for it, such as
'whence could' and 'tale so'. In this context only the setting of
'wretches' is questionable. Purcell's sensitivity to word rhythm
reminds one of Lawes's similar awareness and concerns.

Like Locke, however, Purcell also writes florid declamation.
And like Blow, he attaches these melodic decorations to the
words they are meant to describe. Thus, for 'storms' he makes the
line leap down a fifth and tear back up through an octave. For
'valour' he uses the pomp of dotted notes in a turn figure. 'Fierce'
calls upon a rising line similar to 'storms' but ascends a fifth higher
and is pitted against a resolutely descending bass.

In addition to this attention to single words, the whole
declamation is tied together harmonically. Moreover, the harmonic progression not only makes perfect tonal sense, but it
reflects the dramatic situation. As Dido initiates the discussion
with the rather helpless question 'Whence could so much virtue
spring?', the harmony remains without motion on a C minor

chord. In the second line, as she recalls Aeneas's stories of the
Trojan war, her excitement grows, the vocal line rises even
higher, and the harmony shifts in two quick moves into the more
resolute G major. After turning to C major for 'Anchises' valour',
the third line shifts to the flat side for Venus's softer charms (F
major). The fourth line takes the listener back to C minor for
'how soft in peace' and cadences to C major on 'how fierce in
arms'. This first section thus centres around C major-minor.
Dido's torment and Venus's charms are reflected by the flat and
minor chords; Aeneas's might and Anchises's valour by the sharp
and major chords. But the C harmonies dominate throughout,
and the four lines cadence respectively to the minor tonic, the
major dominant, the major subdominant, and the major tonic.

Belinda enters speaking of Aeneas's story being able to 'melt
the rocks' as well as Dido; she moves into the new key of G
minor, both a flat and a minor key. With a sudden and
unprepared deflection to an E flat major chord, the second
woman sings of an unmoving, 'stubborn heart'. The use of a
major tonality and its unprepared arrival depict just such 'stub-
bornness' untouched by the preceding G minor. The second
woman's line ends on G major.

In concluding the song, Dido sings only of her own emotions.
The five lines left to her close on flat or minor chords: B flat
major, E flat major, F major, E flat major, and C minor.
Throughout the song these have represented the softer and more
susceptible emotions; they depict Dido's distress. C major and G
major—both 'hard' keys—are conspicuously absent from this
section.

This analysis illustrates that 'Whence could so much virtue
spring?' is not a simple recitative but a carefully and strictly
measured declamatory song. It is stable within the key of C
minor, in which it begins and ends, and the melody is heightened
with florid ornamentation. The regularly recurring rhymed
couplets of the text also add to the song-like quality. To perform
this or similarly composed sections of *Dido* like recitative by
freely altering rhythms and tempo would destroy the underlying
tensile strength of the composition that plays against the regularity of the beat and harmonic framework.

The roots of this style go back easily to William Lawes and
even further to Robert Johnson; Ian Spink writes of a 'direct line

that leads from Lanier to Purcell'.[32] The major distinction between previous declamatory airs and Purcell's lies in the sophistication of harmonic methods and in the highly-developed dramatic quality of the later composer's work. Purcell, of course, learned a great deal from the achievements of Matthew Locke and John Blow, but he was able to take attention to word accent, florid declamation, and harmonic organization and turn them all to the communication of an emotional text. The division of the vocal line among three participants adds to the dramatic quality, but it does not alter the compositional style or its heritage. It is the genius of Purcell that he saw the latent dramatic potential in the declamatory air and used it in a somewhat untraditional way. *Dido and Aeneas* is proof of his achievement.

Throughout the opera Purcell uses only the traditional English song forms—the declamatory air, the dance or tuneful air (with or without a repetitive bass), the two-part air (which begins with a section in declamatory style and ends with a section in tuneful style) and the dialogue (which begins with dialogue in declamatory style and ends with a simultaneous duet in tuneful style). Sometimes certain concessions are made to the dramatic situation, but the succession of instrumental pieces, solos, and choruses remains just as it had been in Lawes's *The Triumph of Peace*.

The section beginning 'Grief increases by concealing', for example, clearly comprises a two-part air. The opening declamatory part is shared by two singers in alternation—a dramatic necessity—and cadences typically to the dominant. The second and tuneful part ('The greatest blessing fate can give') returns to the tonic.

The song 'Ah, Belinda' offers another, and more sophisticated, example of the two-part air that is held together by the remarkable use of a single ground bass throughout. The two sections are strongly demarcated, however, by differences in vocal style. The declamatory section, as shown in Example 9*a* is typified by broken phrases separated by rests and by a jagged rhythmic contour. The tuneful section (Example 9*b*) has flowing phrases with smooth rhythms; it also unifies the bass line with the voice by taking the head motive of the repetitive bass pattern into the vocal part. Each section is also distinguished formally; the first follows the binary pattern AA'; the second, BCB, is ternary.

---

[32] Spink, *English Song*, 118.

Example 9: 'Ah, Belinda', excerpts

The declamation beginning 'See, your royal guest appears' is divided between three singers and has an open harmonic structure, beginning in C major and ending in E minor. Nevertheless, it remains a traditional declamatory air; precedents for such open harmonic plans exist even in self-standing songs outside the dramatic repertoire.[33] In this case, however, the ending in a different key illustrates the disruption caused by the entrance of Aeneas.

In the third act, a declamatory section begun by the Sorceress, 'See the flags and streamers curling' is really a dialogue for the first and second witches, for the Sorceress drops out after her first line. The simultaneous duet section begins with 'Elissa's ruin'd'.

A more typical dialogue musically is that between Dido and Aeneas, 'Your counsel all is urged in vain'. As in the preceding case a third person, Belinda, is given one line but afterwards drops out. The dialogue form here, however, was not inherent in Tate's libretto, as it had been in 'See the flags and streamers curling', so that words had to be added to the 1689 libretto to create suitable texts for the simultaneous duet ending. In the following excerpt the added words, found only in the musical sources, are in italics. It is most likely that Purcell either made or requested these additions in order to be able to use the traditional dialogue form.

[33] Playford's *Treasury of Musick* (1669) contains seven songs by Henry Lawes that begin on a non-tonic harmony. Two of these cadence to unexpected keys. 'A Dream' begins in C major but cadences to F major; it contains the following pattern of structurally important cadences: C–G (as the dominant of C)-F G (as dominant)—C—C—F. By altering a few notes it is possible to rewrite both F cadences to C without damaging the musical flow. Similarly, 'To a Lady Singing' begins in E flat major but cadences finally in C minor. Again, the final cadence can be altered easily to E flat. Purcell's move from C major to E minor is both more daring and more definitive, but Purcell was a more adventurous harmonist, and his declamatory air is not a separate entity. The only other open declamatory section in *Dido*, 'If not for mine', moves more conventionally from the relative minor to major (in the opposite direction of Lawes's 'To a Lady Singing').

DIDO: *Away, away!*   *Away, away!*
AENEAS: *No, no I'll stay,*   *No, no I'll stay,*

DIDO: *No, no,   no, no,   no, no,*
AENEAS: *I'll stay,   I'll stay,   I'll stay*

DIDO: *away, away, away,   away,   away,* To death I'll
AENEAS: *and Love obey, I'll stay and Love obey, I'll stay, I'll stay*

DIDO: fly—if longer you delay.   *Away, away!*
AENEAS: *and Love obey, and Love obey.*

Table 2 illustrates that all of the movements of *Dido and Aeneas* may be analysed in one of the traditional, English song styles.[34]

TABLE 2: *Song forms in* Dido

Vocal section	Song type	Form or style
Shake the cloud	tuneful air	ABA
Banish sorrow	chorus	
Ah, Belinda	two-part air	with unifying ground
Grief increases	two-part air	three voices
When monarchs unite	chorus	
Whence could so much	declamatory air	three voices
Fear no danger	tuneful air	duet
Fear no danger	chorus	
See your royal guest	declamatory air	open harmonic plan
Cupid only throws	chorus	
If not for mine	declamatory air	open harmonic plan
Pursue thy conquest	tuneful air	ABA
To the hills	chorus	

[34] Blow's masque *Venus and Adonis* may also be analysed in this way, although the musical boundaries are more, not less, flexible. The first act, for example, uses the following alternation of musical types: symphony (act tune), declamatory air (à 2), symphony (Hunter's Musick), tuneful air, dialogue, and then a final group arranged as chorus and song (cadencing to E minor) and song and chorus (cadencing to A minor). The act ends with a dance that repeats music from the symphony of Hunter's Musick.

TABLE 2: *continued*

Vocal section	Song type	Form or style
Wayward Sisters	declamatory air	
Harm's our delight	chorus	with short lead-in by 1st witch
The Queen of Carthage / Ho, ho, ho / Ruin'd ere the set / Ho, ho, ho }	declamatory air in two parts with choral conclusions to each	{ part one and first chorus cadence to dom., part two and second chorus cadence to tonic
But ere we this perform	tuneful air	AABB (duet)
In our deep vaulted cell	chorus	
Thanks to these lonesome	tuneful air	AABB′
Thanks to these lonesome	chorus	
Oft she visits	tuneful air	over ground bass
Behold upon my bending	declamatory air	
Haste, haste to town	tuneful air	ABA′
Haste, haste to town	chorus	
Stay, Prince, and hear	declamatory air	two voices
Come away fellow sailors	tuneful air	through-composed
Come away fellow sailors	chorus	
See the flags	dialogue	three voices
Our next motion	tuneful air	AAB
Destruction's our delight	chorus	
Your counsel all is urg'd	dialogue	three voices
But death, alas	declamatory air	open harmonic plan
Great minds against	chorus	
Thy hand, Belinda— / When I am laid }	two-part air	{ first part cadences to dom., second (AABB′) to tonic over ground
With drooping wings	chorus	

In Part I, above, Tate's libretto was shown to be indebted to English literary antecedents. Purcell's style of declamation and his use of traditional English song forms in succession point to a similar indebtedness to English musical antecedents. As with the libretto, a brief look at French and Italian examples underscores this conclusion. The two most influential foreign composers in Purcell's lifetime were Jean-Baptiste Lully (1632–87) and Giacomo Carissimi (1605–74). Notably, both composers were from earlier generations and had died before the time of *Dido*'s composition, but Purcell's style is closer to theirs than to any continental contemporary (such as Alessandro Scarlatti, b. 1660). Nevertheless, the differences are marked.

Perhaps the most famous section of declamation in all of Lully's operas is the monologue from *Armide* (Paris, 1686) where the sorceress argues with herself about her course of action in regard to Renaud (Rinaldo), her former lover. The opening segment of this is given in Example 10. In the eighteenth century the philosopher and music critic Jean-Jacques Rousseau complained that the melody of this declamation wandered aimlessly without regard to the text. Indeed, the repeated arrivals on g″ and e″ in the first eight bars describe a melodic line without tension, without the strong sense of arrival apparent even in the previous examples by Lawes and Blow. Jean-Phillipe Rameau, however, defended the emotive content of Lully's declamation by arguing that the expression lay not in the melody but rather in the harmony — that, for example, the movement under the first sentence to the relative major (E minor to G major) shows Armide's growing strength, whereas her hesitation (bars. 13–14) is depicted by moving away from the major tonic to the subdominant (G major to C major).[35] Whether or not we accept Rameau's argument about the harmonic power of Lully's recitative, it is clear that the declamatory styles of Lully and Purcell differ greatly.

In 'Whence could so much virtue spring', for example, the heroine similarly debates her emotions, but Purcell's florid line bears little relation to Lully's syllabic setting. Compare, for example, Purcell's setting of 'storms', 'valour', and 'fierce' to Lully's setting of 'puissance', 'superbe', 'vengeance', and 'invinc-

---

[35] For an exposition of and detailed commentary on the eighteenth-century arguments surrounding Lully's recitative, see E. Cynthia Verba, 'The Development of Rameau's Thoughts on Modulation and Chromatics', *Journal of the American Musicological Society*, xxvi (1973), 69–91.

Example 10: Armide's monologue from *Armide* by Jean Baptiste Lully, as edited in *Geschichte der Musik in Beispielen*

En - fin il est en ma puis - san - ce, ce fa-tal enne-

-mi, se su-per- be vain - queur. Le char - me du som - miel le liv- re à ma ven-

-gean - ce, je vais per - cer son in - vin - ci - ble coeur. Par

lui tous mes cap - tifs sont sor-tis d'es-cla - va - ge, qu'il é-prou - ve tou - te ma

ra - ge..... Quel trou - ble me sai - sit? Qui me fait hé - si -

-ter? Qu'est-ce qu'en sa fa - veur la pi - tié me veut di - re?

Finally he is in my power—that mortal enemy, that vain conqueror. The charm of sleep has delivered him into my hands; I will pierce his invincible heart. Because of him my captives have been freed, and this has incited all my rage. But what makes me worry? Why do I hesitate? What does the voice of pity wish me to say?

ible'. Also, Purcell's use of dissonant appoggiaturas (note Dido's renditions of the word 'soft', Belinda's 'strong' and 'woe', the Second Woman's 'distress', and finally Dido's chromatic ascent on 'but, ah!') contrasts with Lully's triadic melody.

There are differences harmonically as well. Purcell's harmony reflects the drama through the use of key identification at the level of the scene, in characters, and also, to a limited extent, in individual pieces. Thus Dido's grief is represented by C minor, and Aeneas is identified by E and A minor. In this declamation, Dido's emotions are presented with flat and minor chords, whereas Aeneas's military exploits appear on sharp and major chords. Lully, at least according to Rameau, uses harmonic motion rather than key identification, moving, for example, to the relative major to depict strength, and to the subdominant to depict weakness. Finally, Lully's harmonic rhythm, typical of recitative, is much slower than that in Purcell's more song-like bass.

Lully's flexible metric structure with its standard rhythmic patterns also differs markedly from Purcell's metric regularity that underlies an extraordinary rhythmic freedom. That is, Lully's recitative follows the French convention of setting verse quantitatively in long and short syllables in the ratio of two to one. Thus in the phrase 'il est en ma puissance', the one accented syllable receives a crotchet, all other syllables being set to quavers. With 'ce fatal ennemi', the second syllable of 'fatal' is distinguished from the surrounding semiquavers by (again) being twice the length. The pattern of long and short syllables governs most of Lully's declamation in opposition to Purcell's more accentual setting. In sum, although Lully's recitative is a beautiful and heightened musical composition, its methods contrast sharply with those found in the English seventeenth-century music in melody, harmony, and rhythm.

The same can be said for Italian recitative, although initially the lament from Carissimi's *Jepthe* (*c.*1649) of Jephtha's daughter as she awaits being sacrificed to the gods looks more similar to Purcell (Example 11). The melodic line is clearly song-related and reaches its climaxes coincident with the text—the high g″ coming on 'gloria patris mei' ('glory of my father'), for it is her father who has offered her as a sacrifice, and again at the end of the line as she sings 'morirar et non vivam' (that she goes 'to die and not to

Example 11: *Jepthe*, daughter's lament, excerpt, by Giacomo
Carissimi, as edited by Adelchi Amisano (Milan,
1977)

Alas for my sorrow at the happiness of the people, the victory of Israel, and the glory of my father, that
I, a virgin without child, I, an only daughter, go to die and not to live! (trans. by author).

live'). The melisma on the unimportant word 'et' ('and') also
stands out as reminiscent of Matthew Locke, Carissimi's contemporary. But as in Lully's recitative, the melodic line lacks the
rhythmic vitality (and variety) and harmonic astringency of
Purcell. Indeed what is similar in style to Purcell in this recitative
is similar also to the English antecedents Purcell drew upon, and
what is different is different from these as well. Moreover, the
later Italian operatic recitatives of Cavalli, Steffani and Scarlatti
move away from these song elements that resemble Purcell's
declamation towards a greater and greater reliance on simple

recitation. If Purcell knew this contemporary Italian style (*recitativo semplice*) he rejected it for English declamation, and if his music thus reflects the earlier music of Carissimi, the similarity derives from those common musical elements found also in the earlier English declamatory airs. As Anthony Lewis has written, 'such streams of influence as there are from abroad have had to sink well into the ground and be absorbed there before emerging transformed within the flower of Purcell's own style.'[36]

Manfred Bukofzer, in his history of Baroque music, offers a similar conclusion but from a negative point of view.

> The English composers of the early baroque were unable to grasp the essence of the recitative, the affective intensification of the word, and had to find a substitute for it. Like the French, they emphasized the rhythmic factor in the recitative at the expense of melodic contour and harmonic interest. Although similar with regard to rhythm, the French and English recitatives differed with regard to prosody; whereas French composers preferred dactylic and anapestic patterns, the English favored dotted rhythms on the upbeat and such syncopations as occur naturally in 'never' (♪ ♩.). Compared with the Italian recitative those of the early French and English were lacking in pathos and flexibility; they stood on the borderline between song and recitative with too arid and stiff a melody for song and too active a bass for recitative. Not touched by the affective intensity of Peri and Monteverdi they had also little of the spectacular virtuosity of Caccini. What the English composers shared with the Italians was merely the declamatory principle, not its affective application. Only in the middle baroque did composers like Humfrey, Blow, and Purcell infuse sufficient pathos into the melody to achieve affective declamation in music.[37]

Bukofzer was certainly wrong to call English declamation a failure, but he has not stood alone in this judgement. Ian Spink identifies the difficulties critics such as Bukofzer have had in appreciating Henry Lawes; his statement is apt, however, for the declamatory air of the entire century.

> Since his songs derive so much from qualites of speech it is consequently in performance rather than on paper that the full

[36] Lewis, *The Language of Purcell: National Idiom or Local Dialect?*, 21–2.
[37] Bukofzer, *Music in the Baroque Era* (New York: W.W. Norton & Co., 1947), 184.

subtlety and refinement of his technique can be recognized. This is something that critics have failed to grasp. They saw that his style was neither that of recitative nor air but lay between the two. Lacking a name it almost had no business to exist! Harmonically and melodically the idiom was perplexing to them . . . [38]

Bukofzer's criticisms, however, did not affect the clarity of his musical perceptions, for he correctly pin-pointed many of the declamatory air's most important attributes: the rhythmic vitality, the preference for dotted rhythms rather than long-short patterns, and the fast harmonic rhythm. To these we can add the florid madrigalisms and dissonant appoggiaturas of the vocal line, and the harmonic key identifications.

Purcell's compositional style was deeply rooted in English tradition. His attention to word accent in the declamatory air resembles Lawes's, but his more florid style points to the influence of Locke, and the music's integration with the meaning of the text points to Blow. The identification of complete sections by means of a single key reflects all three. Only Purcell, however, uses harmony as a dramatic tool. Although the advance in dramatic writing since the 1630s is obvious throughout *Dido and Aeneas*, the opera's layout also remains essentially the same as that used by Lawes fifty years before. Indeed, one of the most distinguishing features of the English masque preserved in *Dido and Aeneas* is the lack of recitative and aria alternation and the use instead of contiguous song forms.

Of course, it would be foolish to say there were no continental influences working on English seventeenth-century music, for Italian and French styles affected English composition at different times throughout the century. Nevertheless, England maintained in the masque a distinct musical-dramatic tradition of its own, and *Dido and Aeneas* may well be said to be its culmination. We have seen in Part I how closely allied to seventeenth-century English dramatic traditions is Tate's libretto in content, form, and style. The same may now be said for Purcell's score. The song styles, dance styles, general layout, harmonic structure, and musical declamation all derive from and are clarified by the English masque (and antimasque) tradition.

[38] Spink, *English Song*, 86.

8

Ground Bass Techniques

Dido and Aeneas clearly illustrates Purcell's abiding concerns with symmetry and balance. But it illustrates as well that the composer was no mere structuralist. Often Purcell creates a rigid framework only so that he can decorate it freely without fear of imbalance or collapse. In many of Purcell's compositions regularity and irregularity play in this way against one another; in *Dido* such a process appears on every level.

The tonal plan of *Dido*, with each of the six sections falling into one key, has already been discussed. The scheme itself, quite unlike harmonic structures of continental opera, is based on the English masque. But Purcell constructs this seemingly static pattern only to play upon it, such as at Aeneas's entrance in scene ii, or in the witches' scene when the hunt (and its key) interrupts the action. The practice of balancing regularity and irregularity can also be found in the smallest details of *Dido*, as in the irregular 'echoes' of the Echo Dance for the witches. But perhaps Purcell is most famous for his use of such procedures in the middle level of the compositional process, and most specifically in compositions based on a ground bass.

Such pieces have a built-in rigidity; the regularity of the repeated bass exerts an influence over harmony, melody, and phrase structure. Especially strong is the constantly recurring full cadence at the ends of such patterns. Purcell, however, takes these apparent compositional limitations, much as J.S. Bach later treated strict contrapuntal procedures and Beethoven viewed the sonata form, as a base from which his imagination could take flight. Thus Purcell's compositions over a ground bass vary in their working out, and the repetition never becomes a restriction. This can be readily seen in the four such pieces in *Dido and Aeneas*: 'Ah, Belinda', 'The Triumphing Dance', 'Oft she visits', and 'When I am laid in earth'.

The ground bass pattern for 'Ah, Belinda' lasts four bars. Its harmonic implications are clear and unambiguous; in only two cases does Purcell make use of alternate chords (Example 12). In the course of the song this bass is played twenty-one times. Except for two repetitions in the dominant key (the twelfth and thirteenth), the exact harmonic pattern is reproduced every four bars with a strong ending cadence. The lack of variety in such a procedure could easily destroy all sense of forward motion or interest, for to play this simple harmonic pattern by itself twenty-one times in a row would overwhelm the listener with tedium. But Purcell takes what otherwise sounds like a keyboard exercise and transforms it with a melody at once totally integrated with the bass and wholly independent.

His first method involves the use of dissonant non-harmonic tones to push the phrase forward towards resolution. Note, for example, how the strong cadential measure is variously treated (Example 13). In the first instance (*a*) the assumed harmonies are simply and strongly emphasized by placing the root of the tonic six-four and then the leading tone over the two consecutive g's. In its second appearance (*b*), the bass f and melody a′ confirm the implied subdominant chord, but the sonority is quickly coloured by the immediate movement of the a′ to g′. Both the rhythm and dissonance of this motion depict the word 'prest'. And the dissonance resolves to the root of the subdominant just as the bass moves up to g, thus creating a new dissonance. This appoggiatura, continuing the depiction of 'prest', only resolves to the third of the tonic chord when the word changes—to one without affective content. Notably, however, this word change is not synchronized with the movement of the bass; both this and the dissonant melodic tones help to obliterate the persistent regularity of the ground. The bar ends with a dissonant anticipation of the third of the following chord.

Example 12: 'Ah, Belinda', ground bass with simple harmonic realization

Example 13: 'Ah, Belinda', variant settings of the same bar in the ground bass

When this harmonic pattern recurs under the word 'torment' (*c*) Purcell uses similar melodic and rhythmic means, but alters them enough for a clear distinction to be made. The bass f is reinterpreted as the third of the supertonic chord so that the dissonant g' can be approached by leap from d", thus distinguishing the sharpness of the 'torment' from the closeness of 'prest'. The bar then proceeds as before but without the final anticipation. Such apparently subtle devices make all the difference in perception; these bars are not heard as repetitive but as wholly different. The higher range in particular and the disjunct motion add to the increased energy level of this second example that belongs to the climactic phrase of the first section.

One additional method of treating this simple cadential pattern also stands out (*d*). Here Purcell neither clarifies the harmonies implicit in the bass nor does he decorate them with rhythmic and melodic dissonance. Rather, by holding a single melodic b' through the bar, he alters both the harmonic rhythm and meaning of the pattern. The first bass note, f, becomes itself an accented passing tone (appoggiatura) rather than a carrier of its own harmony, and both g's support the dominant harmony. Thus the subdominant and tonic six-four chords are eliminated, making this bar not a cadential movement to C minor, but a half cadence itself on G major. Such important changes in the harmonic implication of the underlying bass pattern, however, are not wholly dependent on melodic means, but can better be understood through an examination of phrase structure.

The first (declamatory) section of this song is based on the rhyming couplet:

> Ah, Belinda, I am prest,
> With torment not to be confest.

Purcell does not adhere to this verse scheme, however, but seeks out smaller phrases within the whole. First Dido sings simply 'Ah, Belinda'. The second phrase elides the verses of the couplet—'I am prest with torment'. And finally Purcell gives the entire couplet without break. His three textual phrases are thus of widely disparate lengths. Purcell uses this irregularity to counter-act his repetitive bass.

The first phrase is, like the ground, four bars long. But it begins a bar after the bass begins and, of course, remains out of synchronization. The melody of this phrase plays almost exclusively on the C minor chord (Example 14).

Example 14: 'Ah, Belinda', first vocal phrase

The second phrase, longer in text, also begins on the second bar of the bass pattern but is 'prest' into only three bars (yet another method Purcell uses to portray this word) and cadences with the bass. The third phrase and the third bass statement thus start off together, but this climactic phrase is stretched to nine bars. The intermediate cadences coincide, but the second bass cadence is thwarted by a repeated f' in the melody so that the vocal cadence to C minor comes at the beginning of a new bass pattern. The whole section is then immediately repeated (Example 15).

Example 15: 'Ah, Belinda', final phrase of first section

The second, tuneful section of the song is based on three verses—a new couplet plus a final short line tagging the rhyme of the couplet in the first section:

> Peace and I are strangers grown,
> I languish till my grief is known,
> Yet would not have it guess'd.

Purcell here chooses to follow the verses by line. As in the first section, the first phrase is just four bars long. But rather than beginning a bar after the bass, this phrase anticipates the beginning of the pattern by a bar. Moreover, its first four notes are an exact duplication of the bass at pitch. Here Purcell emphasizes the melodic and contrapuntal nature of the ground; rather than trying constantly to reduce the listener's perception of the bass pattern, he works to heighten an awareness of the compositional process—a tricky procedure at best, for the presence of this bass melody is already overpowering without its transfer to the vocal line. But Purcell thereby effects a *tour de force*, for it is at this point that he changes the harmonic function of the cadential bar by melodic means. By having the voice and bass imitate one another but end out of synchronization, with the melody imposing a new harmonic reading on the ground, Purcell beautifully expresses the meaning of the words he sets. Dido's attempt to capture the 'peace' of the recurring bass melody through repetition is thwarted by an imposed 'strangeness' in the regular harmonic pattern; just as Dido and peace have become strangers, so have the bass and melody lines grown apart. When this phrase is repeated it is elongated to last five bars and thus the cadences finally correspond, but the bass immediately modulates to the dominant for its next two statements—a continuing expression of 'strangeness'.

The next phrase, over the transposed bass pattern, is first stated in four bars; it coincides with the bass. Upon its repetition, Purcell illustrates Dido's increased 'languishing' through melisma, just as the 'grief' had expanded melismatically in 'Banish sorrow' (see Examples 31 and 32). The elongation of this phrase to seven bars elides the bass's return to C and leads without pause to the final vocal phrase of five bars, which provides a final cadence to the tonic in symmetry with the bass. Purcell then repeats the double setting of just the first line of this section ('Peace and I are strangers grown'), giving the whole a rounded structure. Like many great vocal composers, Purcell felt free to take such liberties with his given text. And by use of such means Purcell evolves a tightly knit melodic structure over the twenty-one statements of his ground bass.[39]

The first section, repeated exactly (AA), is set in rather free declamation; the second, in song style, presents a rounded form (BCB). The bass serves not as a redundant and mechanical facet of the composition but as the thread that ties it all together. Moreover it does not persist independently but is interwoven with the vocal line as a partner in the communication of the text.

Thus we can see how Purcell blends regularity and irregularity. The bass is strictly repetitive. The vocal line is often asymmetrical in regard to this line but completely regular within its own pattern (AABCB). And both patterns are made to combine, if not always coincide, in an entity that surpasses them both.

These techniques serve Purcell in many of his ground bass compositions, although their use depends always on the situation. The Triumphing Dance, for example, is far more regular than

---

[39] In an example from a different period, Franz Schubert ends 'Gretchen am Spinnrade' with an added statement of the refrain, thus concluding with a sense of hopelessness rather than, as does Goethe, with the ecstacy of the longed-for kiss.

'Ah, Belinda', but this is explained by its dance function. As in the song, the ground in the dance is four bars long and very simple harmonically; there are twelve statements. The dance melody is rhythmically square as well, and there are few striking dissonances. The phrase structure is the only element of this composition that holds any surprises for the listener.

The first two melodic phrases clearly follow the bass; each is four bars long. The third phrase begins with an upbeat of a beat and a half, and the motion begun here carries through the next bar and cadences to the following bass statement on the dominant. The resulting melodic phrase is thus eight bars long: it elides the intermediate tonic cadence, and ends with the bass squarely in the dominant key. Its expansiveness is then balanced by a musical couplet—a repeated four-bar phrase coinciding with two bass statements again in the tonic. In effect this ends the first half.

The second half begins with a melodic phrase corresponding in length to the ground. There is then a two-bar interlude in the bass pattern, this interruption serving as a long upbeat preparation for yet another eight-bar phrase connecting a tonic and dominant bass statement. Again, a melodic couplet follows in the tonic, and a final single phrase concludes the dance.

Throughout this composition Purcell has taken care not to alter the cadential pattern of his ground; for dance purposes he maintains a regular structure. But he carefully varies his phrases among those of a single four bars, of eight bars, and of repeated four bars. And he builds this variation into a two-part pattern that helps shape the movement on a broader scale than the bass might otherwise allow. The only irregularity he permits is the two-bar interlude in the second part, an elongation device familiar from 'Ah, Belinda', especially as Purcell at this point transfers the ground bass into the melody. Despite similarities, however, Purcell maintains the dance's balance by avoiding an uneven hiatus. Phrases of three, five, and seven bars suited the style of 'Ah, Belinda', but in a dance they would be out of place. Thus in these two ground bass pieces Purcell adjusts his procedures, similar as these may be, to accommodate the function and meaning of the individual compositions. In 'Oft she visits', which is both song and dance, these methods are combined.

The bass of 'Oft she visits' is also four bars long. Being in running quavers (rather than crotchets) its harmonic implications are more ambiguous and depend on the division of these notes into harmonic and non-harmonic tones. There are thus more harmonic possibilities and Purcell exploits them. The bass is repeated eight times within the song—once (in bars 24–5) with an altered cadence to the dominant—and five more times in the danced postlude. The bass itself is never transposed, and it is never taken up into the vocal part.

The song begins with a full statement of the bass. The voice then enters with a four-bar phrase that matches the bass exactly. This is repeated. So far there has been absolute regularity, but from this point the cadences of the melody and bass do not again coincide until the end of the vocal part. This layout can be investigated through the text.

The first repeated phrase is made up of a rhyming couplet:

> Oft she visits this lone mountain
> Oft she bathes her in this fountain.

that describes a regular practice of Diana, goddess of the hunt. The text goes on to recall how on one of these occasions young Actaeon accidentally witnessed the ritual and was turned into a stag by the angry goddess and killed by his own dogs. By invading Diana's privacy Actaeon's life was shattered. Thus as the ritual, represented by the ground bass, proceeds, the literal dismantling of Actaeon's life is portrayed in the voice. The phrase 'Here Actaeon met his fate' takes only three bars, cadencing nevertheless to the tonic, D minor. Its repetition takes only two and a half bars and cadences to G major. The next phrase, 'pursu'd by his own hounds', lasts two bars and ends on A major as the dominant of D, but the condensation of phrase length reaches its ultimate with 'And after mortal wounds' taking but one and a half bars, cadencing to B flat major. At this point the elongation process begins musically and textually. The last phrase is repeated with the addition of 'discover'd too late'. It lasts four and a half bars and cadences to the dominant, A major, with an intermediate cadence in the bass that briefly tonicizes A minor. This whole phrase is then repeated with the addition of 'here Actaeon met his fate. The final phrase lasts six bars and cadences, like the first phrase of the section, to D minor.

Note the circular and asymmetrical text of this second part:[40]

Here Actaeon met his fate,   (1)
Pursued by his own hounds,   (2)
And after mortal wounds,   (3)
Discover'd too late,   (4)
Here Actaeon met his fate.   (5)

The repeated line creates a textual hiatus after 'hounds' that is musically identified with an important half cadence on the dominant. The central rhyme (hounds–wounds) thereby joins two separate grammatical phrases, and Purcell mirrors the textual disjunction between the rhyme and phrase structure by setting his melody and bass at cross purposes. In Figure 2, the melodic and bass phrases are shown with their cadential points, and the poetic line is given in parentheses (by number). Only the second half of the song is illustrated. Paralleling the five lines of the poem occurring in rhymed regularity, Purcell uses five repetitions of the bass. The melodic phrases do not coincide with this pattern, however, just as the sentence structure does not coincide with the rhyme but takes off on its own. The musical result is a particularly free melody, almost improvisatory in feeling.

When the song ends, however, and the danced postlude begins, utter regularity returns; the cadences of the melody and bass always correspond. First there is a repeated four-bar phrase (AA), then a single four-bar phrase with the bass deflected to an F major cadence (B), and then another set of paired phrases in D minor (CC).

FIGURE 2

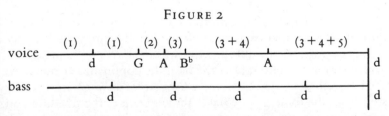

[40] The repetition of the first line at the end of this section of the text does not occur in the 1689 libretto. Unlike the line repitition in ' Ah, Belinda', however, where the textual refrain supports a musical refrain, the repeated line in 'Oft she visits' becomes an integral part of the musical fabric. Also unlike the refrain in 'Ah Belinda', the textual repetition in 'Oft she visits' is added to the 1700 libretto and all later sources. One may assume it derives from Tate himself rather than from a second hand.

In sum, Purcell begins this song in a rigidly symmetrical manner for three bass statements. The middle section of five statements takes melodic flight and thus mirrors both the structure of the text and its meanings. In the last danced section symmetry returns with an extended repetitive pattern overlaid upon the four-bar bass. Both the second and third sections, moreover, are organized by carefully controlled harmonic returns. Many of Purcell's methods for dealing with ground basses may be found here, and his careful juxtaposition and often superimposition of regularity and irregularity is masterful. But the end result does not produce an integrated whole; the sections seem unrelated on the larger plane despite the repetitive bass, a fault not found in either 'Ah, Belinda' or 'The Triumphing Dance'. Even these compositions, however, cannot compare to the masterwork of the opera—Dido's final lament, 'When I am laid in earth'.

The very ground of the lament sets it apart from all others in the opera. First of all it is five bars in length, in itself antithetical to regular phrasing, but even more important to its profile is the chromatic descent through the upper fourth of the scale and the cadence by leap to the lower octave (in G minor). These two distinct parts of the ground, the chromatic descent and cadence shown in Example 16, divide it equally into balanced halves.[41]

Example 16: 'When I am laid in earth', ground bass

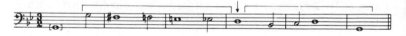

The voice enters after one full statement of the bass pattern. Purcell takes the first two lines ('When I am laid in earth may my wrongs create/No trouble in thy breast') and sets them so that each ends on the central D of the bass, the dominant harmony. As the bass resolutely descends, these lines strive upward, moving by step from the tonic g' to e flat", above. Despite the freedom and breadth of the phrase structure (nine bars divided into four plus five over bass repetitions of five bars), little symmetries in the

[41] See Ellen Rosand, 'The Descending Tetrachord: An Emblem of Lament', *The Musical Quarterly*, lxv (1979), 346–59, for a discussion of the traditional association between the kind of ostinato bass found in 'When I am laid in earth' and the lament. In Italy this relationship was formalized by the end of the 1640s.

vocal line tie the entire nine-bar statement together (Example 17). The entire section is repeated exactly.

The second section begins with repeated outbursts on d″, and the line continues to hover around this note as if unable to continue the upward ascent begun in the first part. But suddenly on Dido's third and last heart-rending 'remember me' it breaks through by leap to the high g″ and floats down diatonically through the octave to the song's starting-point, cadencing for the first time with the bass in G minor. This section, too, is repeated, but initially it is differently aligned with the ground. The change helps to portray Dido's distraction in her last moments and helps, too, to build the necessary tension for the repeated climax on the high g″.

Example 17: 'When I am laid in earth', first vocal phrase

The scope given in this piece to Dido's last words would be treasure enough—the extended phrases, the struggle apparent in the rising melodic line, the small repetitions sometimes aiding the inner wholeness of the line, sometimes building tension, and the large-scale repetitions giving the whole a broader framework—but Purcell completes his masterpiece with the surrounding sections that raise the composition to a still higher plane.

Dido's previous declamatory section beginning 'Thy hand, Belinda' is tied closely to the lament. Starting on c″ it descends chromatically through to d′—moving from the subdominant of G to its dominant, from a fourth above to the fourth below the tonic (Example 18). The half cadence to D major at the end of the declamation leads to the lament in G minor, following the pattern of most two-part airs that cadence first to the dominant and then to the tonic. The bass melody that follows this half cadence, then,

Example 18: 'Thy hand, Belinda', vocal part

derives its chromatic, descending motion from the preceding
vocal line. The entire octave, however, is still not given chromatically but interrupted at its midpoint, d, just as the declamation
had ended on d'. During the lament Dido resolves this octave
downward, but she does so diatonically—perhaps we could say in
human terms. The heavenly transformation occurs in the instrumental epilogue where, as Dido expires, the full chromatic G
minor scale finally is given, not in the bass, but in the treble
(Example 19). This is certainly one of the most sublime moments
in the opera. It should be noted parenthetically that the concluding chorus, 'With drooping wings', continues the descending
scalar motion from g" to g', but like the living Dido the courtiers
express themselves diatonically. The one chromatic descent is
unique and reserved for a special moment.

   In this two-part air 'Thy hand, Belinda'—'When I am laid in
earth', Purcell achieves total mastery over the complex relationship between regular and irregular musical elements. The ground
bass repeats strictly while the vocal phrase structure freely varies.
Yet the vocal line adheres to a larger but regular repetitive
scheme, and the reason its cadences consistently overlap with
those of the bass is largely because the ground itself is irregular in

Example 19: 'When I am laid in earth', melody of instrumental
        postlude

length. The ground is previewed by the declamatory section that precedes the air; the fulfilment of the entire chromatic scale, however, is reserved for the melody of the instrumental postlude. One senses a meaning in these structures that rises above technique. Purcell uses the chromaticism first as Dido speaks of her impending death. It then lurks under her final words to Belinda— the unyielding repetitions seem to bespeak the fate she asks Belinda to forget. And as Dido completes her requests the vocal line coincides with the fate motive for the first time—Dido and her fate finally touch, and she dies. At the moment fate is fulfilled, the chromatic scale, raised from its subterranean depths, is completed as well.

Perhaps this analysis is too fanciful, but Dido's lament in some way approaches the metaphysical. Like the metaphysical poets of the previous generation Purcell here and elsewhere interweaves passionate emotion and rational thought. His musical method involves the *simultaneity* of regularity and irregularity.

Anthony Lewis has quoted a description of John Donne's ('metaphysical') poetry as particularly applicable to Purcell's music:

> He is one of the first masters, perhaps *the* first, of the elaborate stanza or paragraph in which the discords of individual lines or phrases are resolved in the complex and rhetorically effective harmony of the whole group of lines.[42]

This process of small discord resolved within the larger whole can be seen throughout *Dido and Aeneas*—from the smallest musical detail to the highest structural level. In his ground bass compositions Purcell focuses specifically on this technique of balancing regular and irregular elements to a dramatic and musical end. Although some of his techniques are recognizable from piece to piece, the individuality of each is clearly projected, and Dido's lament in particular merits special praise. This process, however, may be seen throughout the opera as Purcell yokes the disparate elements of his craft (often miraculously) to a single purpose—the composition of music that rises above simple accompaniment of the text to become the active embodiment of the drama.

[42] Herbert Grierson, quoted by Lewis in *The Language of Purcell*, 8.

Part III

Performance History

Introduction to Part III

After the performances in 1689, 1700, and 1704, *Dido and Aeneas* lay dormant for some time. The first revivals, documented by dated programmes of the Academy of Ancient Music, took place on 21 April 1774 and 22 February 1787. Textual alterations from the earlier versions help to associate with these performances specific musical manuscripts, one of which (British Library Add. MS 31450, dated 1784) carries the notation that it was copied for the 'Concerts of Ancient Music', a designation that will be discussed more fully below. This set of manuscripts preserves the many musical alterations made in Purcell's score for the late eighteenth-century performances.

After the Academy productions, *Dido* suffered an even longer dormant period only to be revived in the late nineteenth century. With these performances *Dido* started to make its modern reputation, and the growing popularity of the opera can be witnessed in the proliferation of editions, recordings, and national premières. These illustrate further a performance history that moves from being apologetic (using altered versions and augmented orchestral parts) to an understanding of the value and beauty of the original score—a movement for *Dido* that was spearheaded by contemporary English composers.

Part III, therefore, offers a study of the performance history and reception of *Dido and Aeneas* beginning with (1) the late eighteenth-century performances of the Academy of Ancient Music, whose sources will be examined for alterations made in the text and music. Following chronologically, it will be possible to investigate (2) the nineteenth-century revival, which comes at the time of *Dido*'s two-hundredth anniversary, and (3) the twentieth-century performance trend towards authenticity. Finally, an annotated appendix offers an overview of the performance history of *Dido and Aeneas* as seen through national premières, editions, and recordings.

9

The Late Eighteenth-century Performances

The Academy of Ancient Music was founded in the early eighteenth century (the exact date differs in various accounts) by a group of professional musicians hoping to resuscitate older music, which originally was taken to mean that composed before the start of the seventeenth century. But clearly this definition changed with time. A book preserved at the British Library, entitled *The Words of Such pieces as are most usually performed by the Academy of Ancient Music, 2nd ed.* (London, 1768), includes separate sections devoted to Purcell and Handel, and these are the only two composers so honoured. The Purcell section, while containing such stage works as *King Arthur* and *The Indian Queen*, lacks *Dido and Aeneas*. Although few programmes survive from concerts given by the Academy, one can conclude on the basis of this wordbook that *Dido* was not performed by the Academy before 1768. Thus the programme from 1774 attesting to a full performance of the opera may represent its first performance since 1704. In 1787 the opera was again performed along with short pieces by other 'ancients', such as Handel, Stradella, and Pergolesi. There is no evidence of any further performances before the Academy disbanded in 1792.

In 1776, however, another group, the Concerts of Ancient Music, had sprung into existence with the aim of not performing any music less than twenty years old. By 1785 these concerts had gained the patronage of George III, and it seems safe to assume that the success of this organization helped to undermine the earlier Academy. It also seems likely that the two groups were associated in some way. This is indicated not only by the notation on BL Add. MS31450 that it was copied for the 'Concerts of Ancient Music', whereas its performance can clearly be associated with the Academy, but also, in a more general way, by the love these performing groups shared for the music of Handel. Both performed his music extensively, and it is probably no coincidence that the last president of the Academy, Dr Samuel Arnold, was also the editor of the first Handel edition (1787–97).

The Concerts of Ancient Music continued until 1848, and an inventory of its library preserved at the British Library, *A Catalogue of the Musical Library belonging to His Majesty's Concert of Antient [sic] Music* (London, 1827), shows an expanded Purcell section now including *Dido and Aeneas*, perhaps the very manuscript described above. Because complete sets of programmes survive for the organization, it is possible to know, however, that *Dido* was never performed in its entirety by this group. In fact, the only composition from the opera to appear on its programmes was the duet 'Fear no danger'—which was sometimes sung as written and sometimes performed as a trio with a bass doubling the continuo line. Indeed, it appears with startling regularity: 1780 (twice), 1781, 1782, 1783, 1785, 1786, 1788 (notice that it was not performed in 1787, the year the Academy put on a complete performance), 1789, 1795, 1798, 1800, and then every year until 1822 (twice in 1815), 1827, 1829, 1835, 1837, and 1838. Is it any wonder that by 1803 complaints were lodged against these concerts for 'want of variety'?[1]

Although there are no known performances of *Dido and Aeneas* in the early years of the nineteenth century, manuscript parts of the opera survive at the Royal Academy of Music that are dated 1807 and 1817. These may represent performances that cannot at this time be documented. After these dates, there is no evidence of any performance until the late nineteenth-century revivals.

Late Eighteenth-century Sources

Two eighteenth-century librettos attest to performances of *Dido and Aeneas* by the Academy of Ancient Music. The earlier one, dated 21 April 1774, is preserved at the New York Public Library. The other, from 22 February 1787, survives in a bound volume of programmes that includes full texts for all of the Academy's performances in that year and is preserved in the Portraits Room of the Royal College of Music.[2] The 1774 libretto is fully titled—

---

[1] See *The New Grove's Dictionary*, 'London', vol. 11, 194.
[2] Very few programmes from this Academy seem to survive. The only others that I

'The Loves of Dido and Aeneas: An Opera written by Nahum Tate, Esq. and set to music by Mr. Henry Purcell performed, with several other pieces by the Academy of Ancient Music on Thursday, April 21, 1774'—a description that is borne out by what survives of the programme.

Act I

Ode—Benjamin Cooke
Dido and Aeneas—Henry Purcell
Anthem—Dr. Howard

Act II

Glee—Benjamin Cooke
Motet—Signor Negri

Sandwiched between two shorter pieces in the first half of the evening's entertainment, *Dido* assumes no position of importance. The complete 1787 programme illustrates a similar ordering (see also Plate 6).

Act I

Overture, Pharamond—Handel
Madrigal. Chlori son fido—Stradella
Duet. Cease thy Anguish—Handel
Anthem. I heard a great Voice—Dr. Cooke
Glee. When Sappho tun'd—Danby
Motett. Domine ad adjuvandum—Pergolesi

Act II

Concerto ed, Op. 4ta—Avison
Glee. Hark! the Lark—Dr. Cooke
Masque. Dido and Aeneas—Purcell
Full Anthem. My Heart is inditing—Handel

These programmes suggest that the opera was performed in concert version and, in all probability, from beginning to end without a break, and, of course, without the Prologue. Information derived from the librettos themselves tends to confirm these performance conditions.

---

know to exist belong to the British Library and represent only the following performances: 24 April 1746, 6 April 1749, 28 February 1751, 29 April 1756, 5 May 1757, 30 April 1761, and the textbook for Handel's *Messiah* performed in 1761. Perhaps, then, the Academy programme book at the Royal College is the only one surviving that covers an entire year.

The 1787 libretto points to a continuous performance by having no explicit act divisions, and the numbering of the scenes, different from that in all previous sources, is appropriate to a non-visual or concert version. That is, the demarcation of scenes is no longer dependent on changes in backdrop as it had been in the 1689 libretto—Act I, the palace; Act II, scene i, the cave; Act II, scene ii, the grove; Act III, the ships—but is determined as in contemporary Italian operatic practice, by the arrival of a new character. Therefore, the first act begins with the entrance of Dido and her attendants, but a second scene is indicated at the entrance of Aeneas, a third at the entrance of the Sorceress, and a fourth at the entrance of the witches. At the next entrance, that of Dido, Aeneas and their attendants, there is no scene number given, but the Spirit's entrance, which immediately follows, is labelled scene ii. This implies that an act division was assumed at the entrance of Dido *et al.* even though none was indicated, and the reappearance of the designation scene i at the entrance of the sailors, following the scene with the Spirit, confirms yet another act division. These three acts, implied by three sequences of numbered scenes, correspond exactly with those in the Tenbury manuscript: scenes i to iv in the 1787 libretto relate to the palace and cave scenes, the next [i] to ii to the grove, and the final i to iv to the scene at the ships. Thus when the 1787 libretto states at the outset that the opera was 'Divided originally into Three Acts', it refers only to the lopsided division of the Tenbury source, not to the divisions of the libretto. In fact, it seems clear that the editors of this version had only the Tenbury score—or one just like it—to depend upon. Not only are the act divisions still identical, but the 'missing' material at the end of Act II is still lacking, and the changes to the text, discussed above, are all replicated. In fact, the title of the 1774 libretto repeats that of the Tenbury score, 1700 playbook, and 1704 advertisements as well—'The Loves of Dido and Aeneas'. The textual sources, however, do not seem to have influenced these later librettos at all, and there are also enough alterations to separate the Academy performances from the Tenbury manuscript. That is, the late eighteenth-century librettos define a version different from all prior productions.

In Tate's libretto Belinda is Dido's attendant. She had replaced Anna, Dido's sister, in Virgil's *Aeneid*. In the Academy libretto, Belinda reverts to Anna, and the change is consistently made in character designation and text. Thus Dido's air 'Ah, Belinda' becomes 'Ah, my Anna'. And Dido's recitative before the final lament changes from 'Thy hand, Belinda' to 'Thy hand, my Anna'. Even the relationship is clarified. Where Belinda marks Aeneas's final entrance with 'See, Madam', Anna sings, 'See, Sister'.

Another major change occurs at the problematic ending to Act II. The chorus and dance from Tate's libretto for which no music survives is not included, but even Aeneas's monologue is cut to include only one couplet.

> Jove's commands shall be obey'd.
> Tonight our Anchors shall be weigh'd.

This reduction allows Aeneas no vacillation or self-doubt.

The comparison of these librettos to the Tenbury score also reveals that the dance element is reduced—consistent with a concert performance. 'The Triumphing Dance', 'Echo Dance', and 'The Witches' Dance' (originally 'Jack of Lanthorn' panto-mime) are all lacking; even the opening Ritornelle of the Grove scene is omitted. The only indication remaining for an independent dance movement is that for 'The Sailors' Dance' after the chorus 'Come away, fellow Sailors'. These omissions of declamation and dance would probably limit the duration of the opera to no more than forty-five minutes—an appropriate length for a choral work comprising part of an evening's music programme.[3]

Minor changes of word throughout the librettos, although not of structural importance, also help to associate the Academy librettos with their scores. In 'Ah, Belinda', 'confest' is changed to 'express'd', and in Aeneas's declamation after the hunt, 'those did Venus' huntsmen' becomes 'those *that* did Venus' huntsmen'. The Spirit's message now refers to the 'Latian shore' not 'Hesperian shore', and the Sorceress calls to her 'Weird Sisters', not 'Wey-ward Sisters'.[4] Finally, where Belinda in the final dialogue

---

[3] Other cuts are visible in the music: (1) the repetition of the opening section of 'Ah, Belinda', (2) the repetitions of both sections of 'When I am laid in earth', (3) the repetition and any indication of first and second endings in the Sailors' Dance, (4) the repetitions in the first section and danced postlude to 'Oft she visits', and (5) the echoes in 'In our deep vaulted cell'.

[4] The eighteenth-century adapters aimed partly at restoring the classical foundation to the Dido legend and thus Belinda reverts to Anna. The alteration of the Sorceress's text

pointed to the abject Aeneas saying, 'See *where* the Prince appears', Anna calls out, 'See the Prince appears'.

All these changes appear in the texts of two scores preserved at the British Library (Add. MS31450 and Add. MS15979), in another score preserved at the Folger Library, Washington, DC (F 770), and in parts preserved at the Royal Academy of Music, London (RAM 25 A and D). These sources (henceforth referred to as the Academy sources) can also be related by their musical content, as will be seen below. All have been tentatively dated to the 1780s, which period can now be confirmed in light of their close relation to the dated programmes of the Academy.

Even though no specific evidence can be adduced, except that the RAM parts contain the dates 1807 (25 C) and 1817 (25 D), it must be assumed that the Academy adaptation of the opera continued to be performed for many years because it was published in this version by G. Alexander Macfarren for the Musical Antiquarian Society in 1841.

The Ohki manuscript, dated *c.*1810, also follows in this tradition.[5] Indeed, the first five pages are in a later, late nineteenth-century hand, and perhaps were copied directly from the Macfarren edition as they correspond exactly: Dido's helpmate is her sister Anna who sings an octave below the Tenbury score in the alto clef, as she does in the Academy scores. And Dido sings 'Ah, my Anna' and exchanges 'confest' for 'express'd'. After these initial pages, however, the most striking resemblances between Ohki and the concert versions end. The alto Anna is transformed back to the soprano Belinda, Aeneas is allowed his complete monologue, and the Sorceress sings of 'Weyward' not 'Weird Sisters'. Nevertheless, the relations between the Ohki score and the Academy versions do not totally disappear at this point. For example, the shore referred to by the Spirit is still 'Latian' not 'Hesperian'; Aeneas still sings after the hunt of 'those *that* did' not of 'those did', and Belinda surprises the listener at the end with 'See, sister', a rather too intimate mode of address for one's mistress. Furthermore, The Triumphing Dance is lacking at the end of the Palace scene (as in all the Academy sources) and is only

---

from 'Wayward' to 'Weird Sisters' may possibly be explained by the same urge, although here the precedent is the witches in Shakespeare's *Macbeth*, who are called Weird Sisters.

[5] For the dating of this manuscript, see Imogen Holst, 'A Note on the Nanki Collection', *Henry Purcell (1659–1695): Essays on His Music*, 129.

inserted after The Witches Dance with no indication of its proper position.

Parallels between various of the earlier sources and the Ohki manuscript imply that it was copied using a compilation of the Academy and Tenbury sources. On 17 December 1877 William Cummings, who owned the manuscript, offered his judgement on the authority of the score as a source.

> This M.S. of Purcell's *Dido and Aeneas* is very curious and valuable containing music which is wanting in the edition published by The Musical Antiquarian Society, and the many variations and differences from the latter copy conclusively shew by their superiority that they are authentic.[6]

And much more recently Imogen Holst has written that 'on the whole the Oki [*sic*] Ms. is the more accurate of the two [Tenbury and Ohki MSS.].'[7] A careful comparison of the texts shows these conclusions to be false. The superiority of the Ohki MS. to the concert version resides simply in its partial reversion to the Tenbury score, but throughout its pages it remains seriously indebted to the Academy sources. The stemma in Figure 3 illustrates the relations among all the sources. That is, the 1689 version can have been the only source for the 1700 adaptation. The 1704 version derived in part from both the altered version and the original sources. The score for this performance, now lost, probably represents the direct source for the Tenbury, Tatton Park, and the Academy sources, all of which were copied within a period of about ten years. Tenbury apparently offers the closest copy of this score; Tatton Park uses modern notation throughout, and the Academy sources have been extensively altered. The Ohki manuscript depends on a collation of a source based on the 1704 performance and the Academy versions.

Musical Adaptation

At least one of the following types of musical changes can be found in all *Dido* sources that post-date the Tenbury manuscript:

---

[6] This note is handwritten on the inside cover of the Ohki manuscript and signed by Cummings, whose bookplate is still clearly displayed on the front cover.

[7] Holst, 'A Note on the Nanki Collection', 130.

FIGURE 3

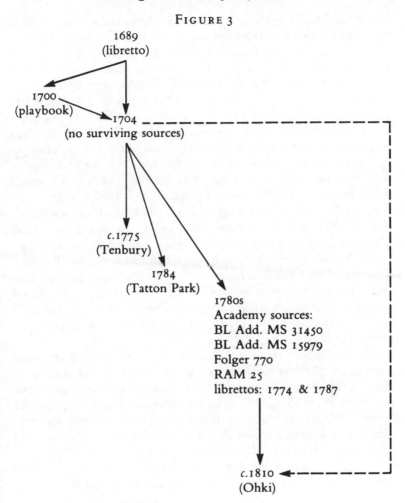

1689
(libretto)

1700
(playbook)

1704
(no surviving sources)

c.1775
(Tenbury)

1784
(Tatton Park)

1780s
Academy sources:
BL Add. MS 31450
BL Add. MS 15979
Folger 770
RAM 25
librettos: 1774 & 1787

c.1810
(Ohki)

(1) the modernization of the notation, (2) the regularization or smoothing out of rhythmic and harmonic elements, and (3) the rewriting of entire passages. Each type of alteration can be discussed in turn.

The modernization of notation is, generally speaking, the least serious of alterations, making little or no impact on the listener, although even it does not always occur without damaging the original intent. The changes include, for example, modernization of key signatures and accidentals. In Tenbury the minor mode is signed in the older way without lowering the sixth degree; thus C minor is written with two flats (B and E), and F minor is signed with three flats (B, E, and A). The modern method of lowering the seventh, third, and sixth degrees in key signatures of the minor mode is followed in all later musical sources—Tatton Park, British Library, Folger Library, RAM, and Ohki. In a similar notational change these manuscripts also follow the modern tradition of having an accidental last through the bar; in Tenbury it pertains only to the single note. Also the natural sign is incorporated to cancel a signed flat; Tenbury consistently uses a sharp for this purpose. And, finally, where Tenbury generally lengthens notes—whether across beats and bars or not—with the dot, the later sources use the tie when crossing a strong beat. Thus ♩. becomes ♩ ♪, but again, these are not differences one can hear. Such changes only emphasize the relationship of the Tenbury manuscript to earlier, seventeenth-century notational traditions and indicate that it may be closer to Purcell's original score than is often believed. With other notational changes, however, Purcell's clear intentions may be clouded sufficiently to cause problems in performance.

All of the later manuscripts consistently modernize the time signatures. Thus where Tenbury uses C and ¢ (or 2), these give only C. And where Tenbury gives 3, they use $\frac{3}{4}$. One might argue that these alterations, too, make no difference to our hearing, for if one is simply counting beats both systems work equally well. But in fact Purcell's use of the older proportional signs indicates more than metre—it also confirms the tempo. The Preface to Purcell's *Lessons for Harpsichord* contains a discussion of metre and tempo that may have been written by the composer himself.

There being nothing more difficult in Musick then [*sic*] playing of true time, tis therefore necessary to be observ'd by all practitioners, of which there are two sorts, Common time, & Triple time, & is distinguish'd by this C this ₵ or this ⏀ mark, yᵉ first is a very slow movement, yᵉ next a little faster, yᵉ last a brisk and airry time . . .

Triple time consists of either three or six Crotchets in a barr, and is to be known by this $\frac{3}{2}$ this 𝅘𝅥𝅮 this 3 or this $\frac{6}{4}$ marke, to the first there is three Minums in a barr, and is commonly play'd very slow, the second has three Crotchets in a barr, and they are to be play'd slow, the third has y^c same as y^c former but is play'd faster, y^c last has six Crotchets in a barr & is Commonly to brisk tunes as Iiggs and Paspys . . .[8]

Similarly, the relationship between metre and tempo in the Tenbury source of *Dido and Aeneas* seems to be based on a strict proportional system.[9] Thus C is the slowest tempo; ¢ (or 2) means a doubling of tempo, and 3 triples the tempo of C. In other words, the duration of the crotchet in C equals the minum in ¢ and the dotted minum in 3 (C ♩ = ¢ ♩ = 3 ♩ .). In ³⁄₈ the tempo of 3 is doubled (that is, one bar of 3 equals two bars of ³⁄₈: 3 ♩. = ³⁄₈ ♩.|♩.).

The tying of this metrical system to tempo is especially clear in the limited use Tenbury makes of separate tempo marks; these only occur when a metrical sign is lacking. For example, the opening of the overture is marked C; at the second section there is no change of metre, but the indication 'quick' is added. This seems to mean a modification of the C without taking the tempo as fast as ¢, for later, in a similar situation, the opposite course is taken. The declamation 'Grief increases by concealing' is in C (as is all declamation in *Dido*), but the connected song-ending, 'The greatest blessing', is given in ¢, truly twice as fast. But then Aeneas's declamation, 'If not for mine' is also in C, and the connected song section for Belinda ('Pursue thy conquest') is marked, like the second half of the overture, 'quick'. Once again, Purcell apparently has chosen a tempo not covered by his proportional metric signs, and he has indicated this by supplying a tempo marking.

The substitution of selected tempo markings for metrical signs implies a need to modify the strict metrical proportions in effect elsewhere in the score. The best example of this occurs in 'Ah, Belinda' where there is no metric marking despite the fact that the metre changes from the preceding duple to triple. The only sign is

[8] Reprinted in Henry Purcell, *Harpsichord Music*, ed. William Barclay Squire, Purcell Society Edition, vol. vi, v.

[9] For a discussion of tempo in Purcell's music, see Robert Donnington, 'Performing Purcell's music today', and 'Further seventeenth-and eighteenth-century evidence bearing on the performance of Purcell's works', *Henry Purcell (1659–1695): Essays on his Music*, 85–8 and 123–4. For discussions of proportional tempos in even later composers, see Arthur Mendel, 'A Note on Proportional Relationships in Bach Tempi', *The Musical Times*, c (1959), 683–5; and Edward T. Cone, *Musical Form and Musical Performance* (New York: W.W. Norton & Co., 1968), 59 (on Beethoven).

the tempo marking of 'slow'. Clearly the proportional sign of 3 would have indicated too fast a tempo and $\frac{3}{2}$ (used for Dido's lament) with 'three minums in a barr, and . . . commonly play'd very slow' is inappropriate. What seems called for is Purcell's 3i which has 'three crotchets in a barr, and they are to be play'd slow'. For some reason, however, the scribe of Tenbury never uses this sign. Thus the marking 'slow' is given without any metrical indication. The situation clearly illustrates that the metrical signs in Tenbury were considered as important, if not more important, for determining tempo as for defining metre. That is, the steady tactus underlying all of *Dido and Aeneas* is only interrupted by isolated tempo markings, and the modernization of the metrical signs, by emphasizing simple metric division, obscures these original and proportional tempo relations.[10]

The proportional metric system of Tenbury is further clarified by the way contiguous movements are elided. For example, where Tenbury dovetails two movements together, clearly indicating the proportional tempo relationships (for example, at the join between the second laughing chorus and 'But ere we this perform', where it is implied that ♩. of the former equals ♩ of the latter), the Academy and Ohki manuscripts separate the movements by elongating the connecting notes and inserting a double bar (Example 20).

Example 20: *Dido and Aeneas*, elision of movements, Laughing Chorus to duet, 'But ere we this perform'

(a) Tenbury

(b) Academy sources, Tatton Park and Ohki manuscripts

[10] See my edition of *Dido and Aeneas* (Oxford University Press and Eulenburg) for a more detailed discussion of proportional tempo relations.

Similarly Tenbury's elision of 'The greatest blessing' and 'When Monarchs unite' is omitted, and the appropriate tempo ratio of ♩. = ♩ is thus undefined (Example 21).

Example 21: *Dido and Aeneas*, elision of movements, 'The greatest blessing' to 'When monarchs unite'

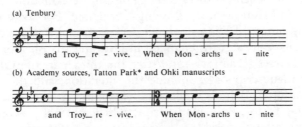

(a) Tenbury

    and Troy— re - vive. When Mon - archs u - nite

(b) Academy sources, Tatton Park* and Ohki manuscripts

    and Troy— re - vive.   When Mon - archs u - nite

*Tatton Park makes only the rhythmic adjustment, not the melodic alteration.

Such examples could be multiplied, but they all point to the same result. Rather than maintaining the brisk and continuous flow of Purcell's original, the later eighteenth-century manuscripts succeeded in regularizing the pattern of movement succession. Due in part to the misinterpretation and modernization of the original metrical signs that were meant to indicate tempo as well as metre, each little segment was given a clear beginning and end so that there might be an orderly procession of differentiated sections. This, in turn, has often led to extreme and non-proportional changes and to a disruption of the somewhat breathless succession of events that leads up to Dido's lament where the action suddenly stops short with the opera's only use of a 'very slow' tempo—$\frac{3}{2}$.

Like the new scenic divisions described above, this alteration attempts to bring *Dido* in line with eighteenth-century operatic practice, where aria and recitative were sharply delineated and each movement was set off clearly from its neighbours. By the end of the century this kind of operatic structure was referred to as 'number opera', since the separate movements were so distinct that they were often numbered in the printed scores. But whereas the modernization of *Dido*'s scenic organization is benign, the alteration to the succession of movements undermines the original

score considerably. All the alterations discussed below as examples
of regularization and rewriting also reflect attempts to modernize
Purcell's score: all are similarly damaging.

The eighteenth-century adapters attempted to smooth out (or
regularize) both rhythmic and harmonic idiosyncracies. Thus the
'Scotch snap' rhythm (♪ ♩.) that has been shown to be so very
typical of seventeenth-century English declamation often is
altered to create a more flowing vocal line. For example, the
opening phrase of Dido's first act declamation, 'Whence could so
much virtue spring?', is changed in both the British Library and
RAM sources (Example 22). After the third bar, the Ohki and
Folger manuscripts also include the alteration, and the changes
continue after Belinda's entrance (Example 23). At this point
even the Tatton Park manuscript, which normally avoids such
rhythmic alteration, adds a variant of its own (Example 24). And
yet there can be no question that the Tenbury rhythms adhere
best to the normal speech accents and thereby enliven the vocal
line more successfully. The Tatton Park variation is particularly
damaging as it creates a strict musical sequence out of Belinda's
first two short phrases and emphasizes the sing-song nature of the
text—something Purcell was always able to overcome and his
adapters to overlook. As a final striking example, compare the
Tenbury settings of two passages from 'Ah, Belinda' to those

Example 22: 'Whence could so much virtue spring', rhythmic
            alteration

(a) Tenbury

Whence could so much vir - tue spring,   What storms,_____

_____ what bat-tles did he   sing

(b) Academy sources

Whence could so much vir - tue spring,   What storms,_____

_____ what bat-tles did he   sing

Example 23: 'Whence could so much virtue spring', rhythmic
alteration

(a) Tenbury

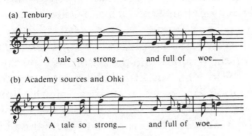

(b) Academy sources and Ohki

Example 24: 'Whence could so much virtue spring', rhythmic
alteration in Tatton Park

found in the Academy and Ohki sources (Example 25). Again,
Tatton Park does not go so far, but it still smooths out some of the
'Scotch snaps' (Example 26).

Example 25: 'Ah, Belinda', rhythmic alteration

(a) Tenbury

(b) Academy sources and Ohki

Example 26: 'Ah, Belinda', rhythmic alteration in Tatton Park

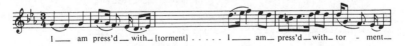

These examples illustrate yet another of the regularization procedures—the tendency to eliminate the harsh non-harmonic tones of Purcell's declamation. Thus in the alteration of 'Ah, Belinda', given in Example 25, the very effective setting of 'torment', discussed previously, is changed to eliminate the dissonant g' on the first beat and the dissonant f' on the initial part of the second beat, while an insipid appoggiatura is added to the last beat creating an exact regularity of rhythmic motion throughout the bar. This essentially consonant flow of even quavers, which actually begins in the preceding bar, is then supposed to depict the expression 'press'd with torment'. It shows instead only how flat the compositional practice of the Rococo period was compared with the Baroque. Purcell's style cannot be easily adapted to this idiom without major losses to the musical interest.

Cadences also fall under the regularization rubric, but the changes take various forms, and some relate directly to those already discussed. In situations where Purcell gives two notes to the final syllable of a phrase, which is a typical procedure, the Academy and Ohki manuscripts alter the phrase to limit the last syllable to one note. Sometimes this falls into the previous category of eliminating an accented dissonant tone (Example 27). But sometimes the change is made simply by altering the text underlay, showing indeed that the two-note ending was a figure especially disliked by the eighteenth-century adapters (Example 28).

Example 27: 'Shake the cloud', cadential alteration

(a) Tenbury   (b) Academy sources and Ohki

Example 28: 'Ah, Belinda', cadential alteration

(a) Tenbury   (b) Academy sources and Ohki

Cadences also tend to be smoothed out rhythmically—following the tendency towards rhythmic regularity seen in the alteration of the 'Scotch snap' (Example 29). And sometimes where the rhythm is already smooth, the later manuscripts still make changes by deleting the anticipation of the tonic, following the tendency towards harmonic regularity (Example 30).

Example 29: 'Cupid only throws the dart', cadential alteration

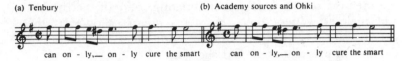

Example 30: 'Pursue thy conquest, Love', cadential alteration

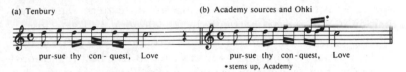

Such situations and cases could be multiplied, for there is hardly a cadence in the entire opera that is not changed in some way in the late eighteenth-century manuscripts, and the pervasive nature of cadential alterations points to a specific category of stylistic change. That is, even though the methods of alteration make use of the kinds of regularization found elsewhere, the cadential situations give a specific character to the changes that set them apart.

In contrast to regularization, complete rewriting tends to occur only in situations that cannot be generalized, and they usually affect some element of Purcell's style that cannot be altered by simpler methods. Thus, for example, 'Pursue thy conquest, Love' is orchestrated for strings in the Academy sources whereas Purcell had carefully reserved string accompaniment of solos to the Sorceress's declamation and Dido's lament. This change, therefore, diminishes the dramatic impact of such accompaniment, but other changes, affecting the compositional structure itself, are of even greater interest.

The Academy scores and Ohki manuscript all work to eliminate Purcell's elongation procedures mentioned in Part II. Sometimes this can be managed merely by changing the text underlay. Thus where Purcell takes the word 'grief' in the chorus 'Banish sorrow' and lengthens it each time it appears (line (*a*), stems up), the Academy and Ohki manuscripts negate the change by adding text (line (*b*), stems down) (Example 31). No musical change has been necessary, yet Purcell's description of Dido's growing grief is destroyed.

Similarly in 'Ah, Belinda' (Example 32), Purcell's depiction of Dido's languishing (line (*a*), stems up) is diminished by reducing the melisma to two bars and eliminating some of the rhythmic and melodic variety (line (*b*), stems down). However, these changes are minuscule compared with what happens to the elongation procedures of 'Oft she visits'.

This ground bass air sung by the Second Woman has been analysed in detail in Part II as an example of Purcell's methods of coping with the repetitiveness of an ostinato pattern. The vocal melody of this song is particularly free-flowing and yet closely adheres to the meaning of the text; in its middle section it follows the bass pattern by having five verses set to five bass repetitions but without any simultaneous endings until the conclusion of the vocal line. Despite its technical virtuosity, however, the piece lacks the coherence typical of Purcell's other ground bass compositions. The Academy adapters attempted to correct this, for in all the Academy scores, this air is given with its middle section completely rewritten (Example 33).

Example 31: 'Banish sorrow', phrase elongation

Example 32: 'Ah, Belinda', phrase elongation

Example 33: 'Oft she visits', a comparison of Tenbury and Academy sources with cadential points circled

*stems up, Academy
stems down, Tenbury

Example 33: *continued*

    A brief glance at the two versions aligned in Example 33 shows
that the eighteenth-century adapter depended exclusively on
Purcell's own musical line, but he shortened it, rearranged its text
underlay, and readjusted its relationship to the ground bass. The
initial statement, 'Here Actaeon met his fate', is given only once,
cadencing to D minor. The next phrase, altered to carry the line,
'Here pursu'd by his own hounds', lasts but a bar and a half, filling
out the length of the ground bass; it also cadences to D minor.
Then Purcell's long melisma describing 'pursu'd' is fully texted
with the three remaining lines, 'And after mortal wounds discover'd too late, Actaeon met his fate.' This rather awkward

setting corresponds exactly with the four bars of the bass pattern and cadences also to D minor. The three verses of this long phrase are then broken down on repetition into two groups of two verses. The first pair comprises the next musical phrase in which Purcell's deflection of the bass cadence to A minor is changed to make this statement, too, cadence to D minor. The second pair makes up the last musical phrase, once again cadencing to D minor but with a strong half cadence to the dominant, A major, in the centre. The interaction between bass and melody can thus be graphed as before (Figure 4).

Purcell's careful scheme is wholly lost; the increasingly breathless shortening of phrases leading to increasingly extended phrases, the constant fluctuation of harmony, and the lack of symmetrical cadences between melody and bass are all missing. In their place one finds regularity of phrase structure, repetitive cadential goals, and absolute cadential symmetry between melody and bass. This middle section thus effects no contrast from the initial vocal section or the danced postlude.[11] Furthermore, the adapters have taken the opportunity to regularize the melody as well.

Note the elimination of the 'Scotch snap' rhythm in the first setting of 'Actaeon', and also on the two–note figure following the first melisma in the original. Of course, the first case also eliminates the appoggiatura a', and, in the next bar, the omission of the g' and f' on 'met' eliminates dissonances there as well, dissonances that certainly are meant to describe the unpleasant clash of the 'meeting' between Actaeon and his fate. In this air, as in all of the eighteenth-century changes, the music suffers a loss of intensity, both in its own drama and in its relationship to the text.

FIGURE 4

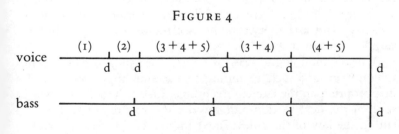

---

[11] Both the initial vocal section and the danced postlude are cut from five statements of the bass to three in order to remove all melodic repetition.

The Academy setting is pleasant where Purcell's had been forceful.

Aeneas's response to the Spirit's commands at the end of Act II provides another example of rewriting. This recitation has proved problematic to modern producers because it ends a section out-of-key and without the strong sense of finality found in other scenes. Apparently, the eighteenth-century producers felt no differently in this regard, and thus Aeneas's response is reduced to its first couplet, and the setting is wholly changed. The underlying reason for so drastic a reaction lay in the changed perception of vocal style from the seventeenth to eighteenth centuries.

Purcell's score, as discussed above, depends heavily on English seventeenth-century musical traditions. As such it consists, like its predecessors, of a succession of airs, choruses, and dances. The airs themselves are of the two main types, declamatory and tuneful, that were equally popular in both song collections and masques throughout the century. Despite its strong roots in the song tradition, the declamatory air was also the closest thing to recitative that the English seventeenth century produced. With the acceptance of continental, and especially Italian, operatic style at the end of the century, England saw the polarization of solo vocal styles into recitative and aria, and the declamatory and tuneful airs were soon reinterpreted as forerunners of the recitative and aria style rather than as two equally important song types. Thus when *Dido and Aeneas* was first performed by the Academy in 1774, its libretto was printed in the traditional eighteenth-century way by distinguishing song from recitative with italic print. In this interpretation not only do the declamatory airs, such as 'Whence could so much virtue spring', become recitative, but integral pieces, such as the dialogue 'Your counsel all is urg'd in vain', are divided into separate movements of recitative and aria (between the declamatory dialogue and the simultaneous duet sections).

Aeneas's monologue was, of course, also judged to be recitative, not air, and such an ending to a section appeared especially inappropriate in the late eighteenth century. The solution was to shorten the declamation and rewrite the remaining segment to end in the key of the sailors' next movement, B flat major. The problems with the previous section are then resolved: the chorus 'Haste, haste to town' concludes the Grove scene in the 'right' key, D major, and the 'recitative' of the Spirit and Aeneas leads directly into the following section dramatically as well as harmonically.[12] However, the crucial dramatic moment of Aeneas's decision, on which hangs the outcome of the entire opera, thereby loses all importance in itself and functions simply as a link from one motion (escape from the storm) to another (preparing of ships). Note the new musical setting (Example 34 and Plate 7).

The first line cadences to the tonic six-three chord. The second line cadences to the tonic in root position. The strong rising line of Purcell's setting, moving purposefully through the octave, is lost, and Aeneas sings in pat little phrases that go nowhere. But more than this difference, Purcell's setting has allowed for Aeneas's ambivalence in that while the line moves up the octave, indicating the spirit of Aeneas the warrior, it ends on a half cadence, showing the pull of Aeneas the lover. Before Aeneas sings of his hesitation, it is expressed by the music. It is Purcell's score not Tate's text, that first makes this indecision clear. By changing the declamation, the eighteenth-century Aeneas becomes even more of a puppet than his seventeenth-century predecessor. And in the process he loses his only song in the opera.

These changes result from a simple misunderstanding about

Example 34: Aeneas's monologue in Academy sources (*a*) compared wih the opening couplet in Tenbury (*b*)

(a) Academy sources

Jove's com-mand shall be o - bey'd. To-night our an-chor shall be weigh'd.

(b) Tenbury

Jove's com - mand shall be o-bey'd. To - night our an — chor shall be weigh'd.

[12] Interestingly, Macfarren waits to end the second 'act' until after the Sailors' chorus in B flat major, but this destroys the integrity of both the D minor-major and B flat scenes.

seventeenth-century musical style—a misunderstanding, however, that has often been perpetuated. Many modern editions still label all solo pieces in *Dido* either recitative or aria, and the strong desire many have to do something about the end of the hunting scene as it has survived derives in part from the perception of Aeneas's monologue as recitative, which it is not, and its position at the end of an act, which division may not be correct.[13] All in all, the eighteenth-century adaptations should teach us that without better information than is available it is preferable to leave what we have of Purcell's music alone. His sense of style, his relation to his period, and his musical genius are difficult, if not impossible, to reconstruct.

Nevertheless, the eighteenth-century adaptations are far from worthless and need not be summarily dismissed. In writing of Restoration adaptations of Shakespeare, including Tate's version of *King Lear*, Christopher Spencer has named three reasons for preserving, if not cherishing, such editions: first, to enjoy them as *new* works apart from the original—some of the delight coming from the author and part from the adapter; second, to learn what the adaptation tells us about the period in which it was written; and third, to learn what the adaptation tells us about the original in terms of an interpretation or analysis.[14]

The eighteenth-century *Dido and Aeneas* can be thoroughly enjoyed on its own merit—compared, for example, with operas of Boyce or Thomas Arne, for Purcell's contribution, however muted, is enough to raise it above the level of most contemporary English scores, while the adaptations fit it to the style of the period. It makes a fine, eighteenth-century English opera. On the other hand, the changes from the original can teach us a great deal about important details of eighteenth-century style, just as they help pin-point what it is that defines Purcell's style. Any document that can aid in such style analysis is important indeed. It might even be refreshing to hear a production of *Dido and Aeneas* as it was performed by the Academy of Ancient Music, for it would open many ears to those stylistic details that typify these

---

[13] If the opera is perceived in two parts, as in Tenbury, then Aeneas's monologue ends only the first section of Part II, just as Dido's monologue ends the first section of Part I. It does not conclude an act.

[14] Christopher Spencer, ed., *Five Restoration Adaptations of Shakespeare* (Urbana: University of Illinois Press, 1965), 32.

two periods a century apart. But just as Tate's *King Lear* will never again replace Shakespeare's, as it did for more than a century, this eighteenth-century adaptation can never again eclipse the unique and beautiful (and seventeenth-century) *Dido and Aeneas* of Henry Purcell.

The Nineteenth-century Revival

After the Academy productions in 1774 and 1787, *Dido and Aeneas* entered a second dormant period that lasted more than fifty years. It seems to have been broken by the first publication of the opera, edited by G. Alexander Macfarren, as the fourth volume produced by the Musical Antiquarian Society in 1841. The sources for this edition derive from the Academy performances, for the text and music match those manuscripts in every detail. The Antiquarian Society, which only existed from 1840 to 1847, was in fact devoted to much the same principles as the previous groups—although it was interested in publication rather than performance. Like three other members on its Council, Macfarren was Professor at the Royal Academy of Music, and this school was one of the first to mount a performance of *Dido and Aeneas* in the nineteenth century. Their production of 1878, however, was not absolutely the first; advertisements stating as much elicited sharp criticism in *The Musical Times*.

> A recent performance of Purcell's [*Dido and Aeneas*] was advertised in the daily press to take place in the concertroom of the Royal Academy of Music. The concert-giver not content to let the opera stand on its own merit, attempted to excite additional interest by stating that it would be the first time of performance since 1677. Several journals in commenting on the Concert accepted the statement as a fact, which speedily brought forward indignant protests from persons who had aided in other public renderings of Purcell's remarkable Opera. The concert-giver at the Royal Academy Room could not plead ignorance of the previous performances, for he was informed of the state of the case before his Concert took place; and it may be well here to record that 'Dido and Aeneas' was one of the stock pieces occasionally performed at the Ancient Concerts. [This is not verified by the extant programmes.] Mr. Cummings possesses a complete set of orchestral, chorus, and solo parts of the Opera, the latter bearing

the names of some of the solo singers—Mr. Dyne, Mr. Bellamy, Mr. Sale, and Mr. Hindle; a tolerably clear indication of performances about 1770–1780. [These took place, as we have seen, in 1774 and 1787.] Coming to more recent times we may refer to performances by the 'Purcell Club,' by the 'Temple Choral Club,' and others under the direction of Mr. E. J. Hopkins. Also to performances at Hackney under the direction of the Rev. J. C. Jackson, also one at Norwood, and another by that well-deserving body, the 'Liverpool Purcell Society,' in 1877. The President of this Society had an impression that the revival of 'Dido and Aeneas' in Liverpool was the first performance since its first rendering under the care of the composer, an error which we now correct, and also that statement that the Opera was composed in 1677. Conclusive evidence has been discussed which fixes the date at 1680.[15]

Of course, the date of *Dido* is now fixed even later, to 1689, and it may be noticed that at the time of this commentary nothing was known of the performances of *Dido* in 1700 and 1704. It is hard to guess the calibre of some of the performances mentioned, since apparently neither the Royal Academy of Music nor the Liverpool Purcell Society were aware of them. Although they were public, they were undoubtedly both local and amateur.

In the same year as the performance at the Royal Academy, the Purcell Society began its publication of the complete works of Purcell, and some of the renewed interest in *Dido and Aeneas* at this time derives partly from the more general Purcell revival that manifested itself in this edition. In 1889—exactly two hundred years after *Dido*'s first performance—the Purcell Society edition of the opera, edited by William H. Cummings, appeared as volume 3 of the complete works.[16] Cummings was able to improve on his predecessors' scores by having at his disposal the original libretto, the Tenbury score (which he dated 1710), the Ohki score (which he owned and dated from Purcell's time), the Folger Library score (which he also owned),[17] and the eighteenth-century performing parts. He writes in his Preface:

[15] *The Musical Times*, xix (1878), 450.
[16] An edition in 1870 by Edward Rimbault was simply a vocal score based on Macfarren's earlier edition.
[17] The Folger manuscript, like the Ohki manuscript, contains Cummings's bookplate prominently displayed.

'Dido and Aeneas' was occasionally performed at 'The Ancient Concerts,' also by the old 'Purcell Society,' and recently revived by the 'Bach Choir,' when the music was performed as here printed.[18]

As stated above, complete performances at the Concerts of Ancient Music cannot be documented by the surviving programmes. Nevertheless, as implied by Cummings's Preface, the Purcell Society edition opened up a whole new era of performances of Purcell's opera. Cummings specifically mentions a performance by the Bach Choir, which took place on 1 March 1888. It would be hard to predict the opera's future successes from the cool reception given this performance by at least one reviewer:

> On the 1st, ult. [the Bach Choir] gave a very attractive Concert in St. James's Hall—one in which variety reigned supreme, represented by a selection of works having the least possible in common. The opening composition afforded its audience a study of the antique, carrying them, for that purpose, back to the days before Handel arrived in England, and in which it seemed that English composers, with Henry Purcell at their head, would succeed in establishing a native school of music. Purcell's 'Dido and Aeneas' is historically too well known for a discussion here of the circumstances under which it was written. Everybody has read the story of its composition, in 1675 or 1680, for performance by the young ladies of a genteel boarding-school. Purcell was then a very young man, and probably worked with none the less ardour because his interpreters were to be engaging young persons of the opposite sex. But it is a pity that he did not associate himself with a better co-labourer than Nahum Tate, whose libretto, though on the ground of decency it would pass muster with Mrs. Hannah More herself, is poor stuff, ill adapted to inspire a composer with noble musical thoughts. Perhaps we ought to blame Tate rather than Purcell when the opera becomes dull, as sometimes it does, but the musician deserves sole praise when, words notwithstanding, his strains rise to the level of their composer's undoubted greatness, as in *Dido*'s death song and the concluding chorus. The opera, of course, can never possess more than an antiquarian interest, but even for that alone it deserves an occasional hearing.[19]

[18] William Cummings, ed., *Dido and Aeneas* (London: Purcell Society Edition, 1889), iv.
[19] *The Musical Times*, xxix (1888), 218.

A year later George Bernard Shaw reviewed a performance by the Handel Society (21 February 1889); and although the performance was apparently not of the highest quality, Shaw at least distinguishes between the composition and its rendition.

Dido and Eneas [sic] is 200 years old, and not a bit the worse for wear ... Henry Purcell was a great composer: a very great composer indeed; and even this little boarding-school opera is full of his spirit, his freshness, his dramatic expression, and his unapproached art of setting English speech to music. The Handel Society did not do him full justice: the work in fact is by no means easy; but the choir made up bravely for the distracting dances of the string quartet. Eneas should not have called Dido Deedo. . . If Purcell chose to pronounce Dido English fashion, it is not for a . . . tenor to presume to correct him. Belinda, too, was careless in the matter of time. She not only arrived after her part had been half finished by volunteers from the choir, but in Oft She Visits she lost her place somewhat conspicuously. [Note that this performance apparently followed a practice begun as early as 1704 of cutting down or omitting altogether the part of the Second Woman, who should have sung 'Oft she visits'.] An unnamed singer took Come away, fellow sailors, come away: that salt sea air that makes you wonder how anyone has ëver had the face to compose another sailor's song after it. . . . I am sorry to have to add that the Handel choir, feeling that they were nothing if not solemn, contrived to subdue this rousing strain to the decorum of a Sunday school hymn; and it missed fire accordingly.[20]

The bicentenary year of Purcell's death, 1895, motivated still more revivals of the composer's works and of *Dido and Aeneas* in particular. The opera was performed in this year for the first time outside England when the University Society of Dublin, Ireland, presented a performance on 14 December. But more importantly, this year saw a fully staged performance—perhaps for the first time since 1704. The score, however, was a far cry from the original; it must have depended on the Macfarren edition of 1841, for the role of the Sorceress, as in all of the Academy sources, was sung by a bass (Mr Emyln Davies), and the Sailor's part was sung by Mr Thomas Thomas, a tenor. It is impossible to tell from the cast list if Belinda was sung by a soprano or alto,[21] but, strangely,

[20] Shaw, *The Great Composers*, ed. Louis Crompton (Los Angeles, 1978), 324–5.
[21] Note, however, that she is called Belinda, not Anna.

Aeneas was sung by a Miss Eva Bedford. Although additional
orchestral accompaniments were added by Dr Charles Wood, the
strength and beauty of Purcell's original shown through to the
reviewer from *The Musical Times.*

> The music is of the kind that exhilirates like the air of a frosty
> morning in spring. It is manly and invigorating in its joyousness,
> tender and expressive in its sympathy, and the very antithesis of
> maudlin sentimentality and frenzied passion. In listening to it—
> and it should be heard for it calls for no great executive means—
> the fact should always be kept in mind that it was written certainly
> five years before Bach and Handel were born.[22]

The reviewer goes on to say that the 'chorus and orchestra did
their work well, under the watchful conductorship of Professor
Villiers Stanford'. One of these choristers was no less a personage
than Ralph Vaughan Williams.

In her biography of her husband, Ursula Vaughan Williams
describes the event.

> One of the great moments of the Autumn term of 1895 was the
> first performance in modern times of Purcell's *Dido and Aeneas.* It
> was given by R. C. M. students at the Royal Lyceum Theatre . . .
> Ralph was a member of the chorus, and because of his height he
> was dressed impressively as a high priest. The make-up man
> refused to believe that he belonged to the ranks and spent most of
> the allotted time in making him up, neglecting the real principals
> in spite of all Ralph could say. He enjoyed himself thoroughly,
> and from then on he and von Holst were firm devotees of Purcell's
> music.[23]

Gustav Holst (1874–1934) and Vaughan Williams (1872–1958)
went on to champion Purcell's vocal music. In 1927, Holst
published an essay on Purcell that illustrated in particular his
respect and admiration for *Dido and Aeneas.* It is titled 'Henry
Purcell: the Dramatic Composer of England', and it is worth
quoting from at length.

[22] *The Musical Times*, xxxvi (1895), 811.
[23] Ursula Vaughan Williams, *R.V.W.: A Biography of Ralph Vaughan Williams* (London, 1964), 43–4. This quotation seems to imply that Gustav Holst was also involved in some way with this performance, an implication I have not been able to verify.

It is generally accepted to-day, thanks to Barclay Squire's researches, that Purcell's most famous opera 'Dido and Aeneas' was written about the year 1689 and not nine years before as was previously thought. Even so it is one of the most original expressions of genius in all opera. Mozart remains the greatest prodigy in musical history, but he was brought up in a fine traditon—in opera, as well as in other music. In England there was not then, nor has there ever been, any tradition of opera. Purcell was first a choir-boy at the Chapel Royal; then he was organist of Westminister Abbey. Yet at the age of about thirty-one he wrote the only perfect English opera ever written, and the only opera of the seventeenth century, as far as I know, that is performed as a whole nowadays, for the sheer pleasure it gives as opera. Throughout the whole work not a word is spoken. Between the lovely airs and choruses there are dialogues, set to easy, free, and melodious music. Probably the English language has never been set so perfectly, either before or since. Playford said of Purcell: 'He had a peculiar genius to express the energy of English words.' There is no chance for vocal display in the ordinary sense of the term, but there is every chance to display powers of expression simply and beautifully.

The opera is accompanied either by strings or by a bass to be filled in on the harpsichord. There is beautiful dramatic and lyrical music, and a perfect sense of rhythm in setting the English language; but it is in the final test of all works of art that 'Dido' stands supreme—the test of unity. Many beautiful works fail in this test—Bach's Christmas Oratorio, for instance. But if you know 'Dido' well, you can feel it as a complete whole. We all know Dido's lament; it is often sung by itself at concerts, but few listeners realize how much they lose by not hearing all that has gone before. It is impossible to appreciate its full beauty without listening to the whole opera and perceiving Purcell's power to make one beauty a stepping-stone to another. Even the Lament is not more moving than the preceding recitative, 'Thy hand, Belinda; darkness shades me', and it is so perfect that only a real master could have added anything after it. Yet how incomplete is would be without the final chorus, 'With drooping wings!'

The libretto by Nahum Tate has been ridiculed for lines such as

> Thus on the banks of fatal Nile,
> Weeps the deceitful crocodile.

But little or nothing has been said in praise of Tate and Purcell for their power to work up inevitably to the final climax. Then, having achieved it, they stopped. What a lesson for the authors and composers of 'Orfeo', 'Don Giovanni', and 'Fidelio'!

Having written a perfect opera—the only perfect English opera—Purcell never wrote or even attempted to write another. He never again set the English language to delightful, free, lyrical recitative (except in certain short works), but fell into dull conventional recitative secco that anybody could have written. Above all, he never wrote another big work with any semblance of dramatic unity. Purcell's 'accommodating disposition' was probably responsible for this. He was at the mercy of his environment.

'Dido' was written for a girls' school in Chelsea. In any good girls' school in any century one would expect to find a certain standard of taste, and a cultivated sense of language. At the same time, as far as dramatic performances are concerned, all stage effects must be severely limited. The singers would be expected to pronounce and to phrase their own language well; but sustained dramatic efforts and any sort of vocal display would be out of the question. 'Dido' meets these conditions to perfection. . . .

It is surely unnecessary nowadays to dwell on Purcell's gift of melody. According to some it is excelled only by Mozart's. Others hold that Purcell's best melodies—and how numerous they are!—are inferior to none. In addition to his gift of melody there are his sense of harmony, his feeling for orchestral colour, his humour, his intensity, his lyrical power. We can witness their steady growth to perfection as we compare Purcell's earlier with his later works. Yet all these details of composition were subordinate to his amazing power of dramatic characterisation.

This power has been possessed by very few opera composers. Indeed, many do not seem to have been aware of the necessity of cultivating it. They have thought it more important to study the idiosyncracies of the particular opera singers engaged for a production than to consider the dramatic foundation on which to build the music. Musical characterisation is usually looked upon as a modern factor in opera. One instinctively thinks of Wagner. Both Purcell and Wagner used all their gifts of melody and harmony, all their mastery of orchestral colour, to give life to their characters and situations. But while Wagner painted huge scenes, each consistent in itself and at the same time part of a vaster whole, Purcell was content to paint little cabinet pictures.

But in one way Purcell is a finer stage composer than Wagner; his music is full of movement—of dance. His is the easiest music in all the world to act. Only those can realise fully the truth of this who have experienced the joy of moving to Purcell's music, whether in the ballroom or on the stage or in the garden; but especially in the garden.

At the end of his life Purcell was master of every branch of musical technique. In all essentials of opera writing, save that of dramatic concentration, he had left 'Dido' far behind. But 'Dido' still remains his one opera.[24]

[24] From *The Heritage of Music*, ed. Hubert J. Foss (London: Oxford University Press, 1927), 47–9 and 51–2. I am grateful to Oxford University Press for allowing me to republish large excerpts from this essay.

II

Twentieth-century Performance Trends

After the nineteenth-century revival of *Dido and Aeneas*, performances of the opera became increasingly more regular, and in this century it becomes possible to distinguish two very important performance trends. The first seems to have aimed at popularizing the opera and making it accessible to modern ears. This trend, which is typified by the use of 'additional accompaniments', began with the Royal Academy of Music performance of 1895 and continued until about 1940. Then the war years apparently caused a temporary break in *Dido* performances, for I have not been able to trace any productions between one in London at the New Theatre in 1941 and another at Sadler's Wells, London, in 1950. But in 1951 two London performances ushered in a whole new era of *Dido* productions, represented by the introduction of *Dido* at well-known houses and festivals, the arrival of the prima donna in the cast, a heightened interest in recordings of the opera, and, most importantly, a growing interest in attempts to perform *Dido* as Purcell might have heard it. This last quality represents the second trend, which rejected rewriting in favour of authenticity. Both trends can be discussed in turn.

Reorchestrations

The 1895 performances of *Dido* at the Royal Academy of Music was memorable on account of its being staged and because Vaughan Williams (and perhaps Gustav Holst as well) was thus introduced to Purcell's opera by singing in the chorus. However, it also started the trend towards added accompaniments. Writing of this performance, a reviewer stated that the early date of the composition of the opera 'was made the more hard to realise . . . owing to the additional orchestral parts, which, with well-intentioned but mistaken zeal, had been written for the occasion

156

by Dr. Charles Wood [a composer and teacher of harmony at the RAM].[25] They were skillfully introduced, but in one or two places those who were familiar with the music missed certain characteristic effects in the vocal parts, which were hidden by horn notes or other obtrusive instrumental phrases.'[26]

In 1924, the first performance of *Dido* in the United States took place at Town Hall, New York, under the auspices of the Society of Friends of Music. Artur Bodansky (1877–1939),[27] conductor at the Metropolitan Opera since 1915, directed the performance using the Macfarren edition with new orchestral accompaniments added by himself. In the same year a performance of this version took place in Homburg, Germany (near Frankfurt) and a vocal score was published—'after the score of the "Musical Antiquarian Society", London, newly edited and orchestrated by Artur Bodansky; vocal score by Gustav Blasser'.[28]

Both the Wood and Bodansky adaptations, then, were based on the Academy version. The Bodansky score not only gives Anna (not Belinda) as alto, and the Sorceress as bass, but all the cuts, melodic alterations, and rewritten passages from the Macfarren edition are retained. When studying the Bodansky score, we may thus keep in mind that the Wood reorchestration was in all likelihood quite similar.

The Bodansky orchestration calls for 3 flutes (1 piccolo), 3 oboes (1 English horn), 3 bassoons (1 contrabassoon), 2 horns, 2 trumpets, 3 trombones, timpani, harpsichord, violins 1 and 2, violas, celli, and basses. These forces are not reserved for special moments or used individually for colouristic detail, but are generally combined and used orchestrally throughout. To take but one example, Dido's lament is already orchestrated by Purcell for the string band. Not content with this, Bodansky uses muted strings, flute, oboe, trumpet, horn, and trombone. And he does not hesitate to alter or add to Purcell's score (Example 35).

That is, under the first vocal phrase, Bodansky doubles the voice with the first violins and adds an echo of the vocal dotted

[25] See the biography in *The New Grove's Dictionary*, 20, 516, by J.A. Fuller-Maitland, H.C. Colles, and Harvey Grace.

[26] *The Musical Times*, xxxvi (1895), 811. Some of the Wood reorchestration may survive in the late nineteenth-century parts (RAM 25 E) for flute, bassoon, and timpani.

[27] See 'Bodansky', *The New Grove's Dictionary*, 2, 834–5, by Michael Steinberg.

[28] Published in Vienna by Wiener Philharmonischer Verlag A.G., 1924. I am grateful to the Music Library of Northwestern University for granting me access to this score.

Example 35: 'When I am laid in earth', as edited and orchestrated by Artur Bodansky (Vienna, 1924)

Example 35: *continued*

but ah! for - get my fate. Re -

- mem-ber me, but ah for - get my fate!

attacca

figure in the fourth bar (of the vocal line) for solo cello. After the first half of the song, which in the Academy versions is not repeated, the trombones enter *forte*, abruptly changing the orchestral accompaniments for the repeated line 'remember me', which phrase is emphasized by added repeated notes in the trumpet and horn, and a new little sighing figure for the flute. The first time Dido sings, 'But ah! forget my fate', she is doubled by the oboe; the horn and trumpet return for the 'remember me' that reaches the high g″; and the flute doubles the voice as it sinks back down to the low g′. Finally, the chromatic octave in the postlude is highlighted by the use of flute and oboe.

Example 35 also illustrates many of the favoured revisions made by the Academy adapters. When compared with the original version (Examples 17, 18, and 20 in Part II) it shows the alteration of melody to achieve a smoother rhythmic and harmonic line (such as at 'may my wrongs'), the internal cutting (neither vocal half is repeated as in Tenbury, Tatton Park, and Ohki), and a full bar added to the end so as to have a complete cadence before the final chorus begins.

It is surprising to find the Academy version so popular more than one hundred years after it was first used, especially as the more accurate Cummings edition had appeared in 1889. Indeed, even the practice of adding new orchestrations can be said to have begun with the Academy adapters, who themselves added a string accompaniment to 'Pursue thy conquest, Love'. The Cummings edition, in one sense, thus represented the first break in the tradition of tampering with (or modernizing) Purcell's score. Perhaps it carried with it an aura of academia that professional musicians avoided.

In 1925 a new edition based primarily on the Tenbury manuscript was published, edited by Edward Dent. At least two of the later reorchestrations are based on this score; perhaps a third is as well. In 1925 *Dido* was premièred in Austria at the Redoutensaal in Vienna, using the Dent score reorchestrated by the composer Hans Gál (1890–),[29] in 1934 this version was also used for the première performance in Holland at The Hague. New accompaniments by the composer and conductor Jenő Ádám (1896–1982)[30] were added to an unknown score when *Dido* was

[29] See 'Gál', *The New Grove's Dictionary*, 7, 90–1, by Conrad Wilson.
[30] See 'Ádám', *The New Grove's Dictionary*, 1, 93, by Ferenc Bonis.

first performed in Hungary at Budapest. The first Italian performance, given in 1940 at Florence, was the Dent score reorchestrated by the Italian composer and conductor Vittorio Gui (1885–1975).[31] This seems to have been the last performance to use a heavily reorchestrated score.

Authenticity

After a break of ten years, encompassing World War II and the recovery period, *Dido* reappeared in London in 1950. In 1951 two London performances set the tone for all that followed: the additional orchestral parts were abandoned and those sections of the libretto that were missing from the surviving scores (notably the end of Act II) were supplied by the addition of appropriate music. The emphasis in *Dido* productions after this time lay in increasing efforts to achieve authenticity.

The first 1951 performance reflects the interest of twentieth-century operatic composer Benjamin Britten in the music of his predecessor.

> At the Lyric Theatre, Hammersmith, on 1 May the English Opera Group opened a three-weeks' season with 'Dido and Aeneas' as edited by Benjamin Britten, who conducted the performance and played the keyboard music on what looked like a spinet. Apart from a duly-guarded realization of the continuo, his editing was mainly concerned with the conclusion of the second act, where there is an obvious hiatus. Mr. Britten says, in a programme leaflet: 'Aeneas sings his very beautiful recitative in A minor and disappears without any curtain music or chorus (which occurs in all the other acts). The drama cries out for some strong dramatic music, and the whole key scheme of the opera (very carefully adhered to in each of the other scenes) demands a return to the key of the beginning of the act or its relative major (i.e., D or F major). What is more, the contemporary printed libretto (a copy of which is preserved in the library of the Royal College of Music) has perfectly clear indications for a scene with the Sorceress and her Enchanteresses, consisting of six lines of verse, and a dance to end the act.' Mr. Britten has supplied a chorus and a dance from elsewhere in Purcell's dramatic music, and the scene is greatly improved thereby as we can all agree. The performance and the staging were acceptable but not distinguished.[32]

[31] See 'Gui', *The New Grove's Dictionary*, 7, 799–800, by Arthur Jacobs.
[32] *The Musical Times*, xcii (1951), 278.

Although the reviewer implies that this performance was interesting only because of Britten's involvement and the added music, the impact it had was far-reaching. In the same year London heard a very 'distinguished' performance that benefited from Britten's work.

> The new Mermaid is a triumph of private enterprise, an Elizabethan theatre raised by a band of enthusiasts in a garden of St. John's Wood, where Kirsten Flagstad came on 9 September to sing Dido. . . . Her Dido, it need hardly be said, was beautiful and moving, expressive in gesture as in voice. Maggie Teyte was Belinda, singing with great artistry and even with a roguish twinkle; her notes might have lost some of their freshness, but they were nevertheless more real notes than those more modern Belindas have produced this season. . . . The musical director was Geraint Jones, who conducted his perruqued band in the stage balcony, while looking-glasses behind the audience reflected his beat to the singers. The chorus was good, the production (apart from the choreography) excellent; future producers might well note Bernard Miles's treatment of the harbour scene, where the chorus 'Come away, fellow-sailors' is sung by the witches, not by the nymphs themselves, who would be 'mourning'. . . . Mr. Miles also included the Prologue to the Opera which appears in the printed libretto, and supplied its dances from other stage-works of Purcell. This libretto, which antedates the Tenbury MS, has strange extra directions (such as Enter the Spaniards, misled by Jack-o'-Lantern), and also the words for the 'missing chorus' which ends the Grove scene. Following Mr. Britten's example, Mr. Evans found music for these lines, but his choice of an *a cappella* chorus hardly seems historically justified.[33]

This performance not only started the competition for authenticity by the dramatic use of the Prologue (which presumably was spoken with dances interspersed, for it does not appear on the recording, see below) and the addition of the numbers at the end of Act II, for which music different from that used by Britten was chosen, but also the person of Kirsten Flagstad brought *Dido* for the first time into the realm of the prima donna and grand opera. In 1953, with only a few changes of cast, a recording of the Flagstad performance was released. In 1960 the Britten score was

---

[33] 'A.P.', *The Musical Times*, xcii (1951), 470.

published, edited by Imogen Holst (daughter of the composer) and Benjamin Britten. In 1975 a recording of this version was released with Janet Baker singing Dido.

In many ways, the performance trend of the second half of this century towards authenticity echoed the late nineteenth-century revivals. In the earlier period, Purcell and his music were resuscitated; in the latter period, the attempt was made to revive the style of Purcell's performance as well. In both periods, contemporary English composers played important roles as they reached back to Purcell and found in him and his music their artistic roots. The clearest expression of this attitude can be found in an essay by composer Michael Tippett entitled 'Our sense of continuity in English drama and music'.

> If through this revival Purcell's music becomes a living though small part of our general European heritage (for among English composers only Purcell can be said to belong to a *living* European continuity), it must form a very important part indeed of our local English heritage. This is not only because of the lack of great names in English musical history, but also because of the spoken language. By this I do not mean so much the obvious fact that music to English texts is naturally closer to English singers; I mean that certain things in Purcell's setting of English words are vital to English composers. For, more than anyone else, the creative artist needs a sense of continuity. . . .
>
> It is unthinkable that composers of my generation, caught up in, if not actual investigators of, the general revival of Purcell's music, should not feel a special sense of continuity with this Restoration composer. Failing an English opera composer as such, Purcell is all that there is. His dramatic music, though incidental, is wonderful in its own right. The general style of his time had loosened the approach to the language, and Purcell had the great gift to make full use of this new freedom, without ever departing from the absolutely natural technique of setting English to music, which had been handed on by the Elizabethans. So that Purcell offers us something the Elizabethans did not possess at all. By the time the next great composer of English is writing, that is to say with the production of Handel's oratorios, the whole scene has gone another decisive change, because Italian has become the universal language for opera; and the English ballad opera has nothing to offer us here. So Purcell stands at the only possible moment in English musical history when a genius could have done what he

did. Since he was this genius our sense of continuity with him, in respect of incidental music for the English theatre, is vital.[34]

Dido and Aeneas, as Tippett writes, is Purcell's only 'true opera', thus its role in the continuity of English drama and music is uniquely special. In particular, for composers eagerly seeking examples of English text-setting, Purcell's declamation became a model. But Purcell's entire musical style, and not simply his style of declamation, influenced almost all modern British operatic composers, and all, in one way or another, became intimately involved with the music of *Dido*. Ralph Vaughan Williams participated in the first staged revival of the work in 1895; Gustav Holst wrote an essay in praise of the opera in 1927, and Benjamin Britten began the move towards authentic performance practice with a production of *Dido* in 1951 based on his own careful reading of the available sources. Finally, in 1959, Michael Tippett summed up this influence in an essay on Purcell's legacy to contemporary composers.

[34] In *Henry Purcell (1659–1695): Essays on his Music*, 42–3 and 45–6.

Appendix: A Short, Annotated Performance History of *Dido and Aeneas*

The growing popularity of *Dido and Aeneas*, the proliferation of performances, and the performance trends, discussed in Chapters 10 and 11, can be documented by looking at the history of the opera's national premières, its editions, and recordings. The premières attest to *Dido's* widening circle of admirers, the editions illustrate the changing performance traditions, and the recordings reflect those changes. The following pages provide annotated lists of these aspects of *Dido's* history.

1. National Premières

After its first performance in 1689 *Dido* was not heard in another city until the Liverpool production of 1877. Shortly thereafter, during the bicentenary year of Purcell's death, it was first heard outside England.[1]

IRELAND, Dublin: University Society   1895

In 1924, *Dido* first left the British Isles (only a little less than 250 years after it was written) in performances using the Bodansky edition.

USA, New York: Town Hall   1924
GERMANY, Homburg   1924

In 1926 it was first staged in Germany in Munster, using Edward Dent's edition. Productions then multiplied, both in foreign languages and English.

FRANCE, Paris: Petite scène   1927
AUSTRIA, Vienna: Redoutensaal   1927
(H. Gál reorchestration based on Dent)
SCOTLAND, Glasgow   1932
HOLLAND, The Hague   1934
(Gál's reorchestration)

---

[1] This list has been compiled from Lowenberg, *Annals of Opera*, from histories of specific houses (such as Dennis Arundell, *Story of Sadler's Wells*), and from reviews culled from magazines and journals (especially *Opera* and *Opera News*). It is an attempt, and nothing more, to indicate *Dido's* foreign conquests. I have little hope that it is inclusive, although I have tried to make it so.

HUNGARY, Budapest   1938
(Ádám's reorchestration)
ITALY, Florence   1940
(Gui's reorchestration based on Dent)

After the war and close to the tricentenary year of Purcell's birth (1959), performances again began to flourish.

SPAIN, Barcelona   1956
SWITZERLAND, St. Gallen   1956
YUGOSLAVIA, Dubrovnik   1956
DENMARK, Copenhagen   1962
SWEDEN, Drottningholm   1962
(English Opera Group in Britten's version with Janet Baker as Dido)

The première in Japan was perhaps prompted by the discovery of the Ohki manuscript in Tokyo.

JAPAN, Tokyo   1968

But *Dido* also continued to make its way around the world without apparent external cause.

BELGIUM, Brussels   1968
EAST GERMANY, Halle   1976

These national premières not only illustrate *Dido*'s growth in reputation, they show as well the move away from the corrupt Academy version and reorchestrations to a reliance on better and more accurate editions.

2. Editions

The first publication of *Dido and Aeneas* was the Macfarren edition of 1841 for the Musical Antiquarian Society. This was based exclusively on the Academy sources. In 1870, Dr Edward Francis Rimbault published a vocal score of this version.

The next edition, by William H. Cummings, was printed in 1888 as 'Novello's Original Octavo Edition' and in 1889 as volume 3 of the Purcell Society Edition. Because he had access to both the Tenbury and Ohki manuscripts, Cummings was able to add the movements missing in the Academy versions and to redress some of the rhythmic and harmonic alterations. Still, the Academy version flourished, and the Bodansky reorchestration (published in 1924) extended its life well into the twentieth century.

In 1925, however, Edward J. Dent published the first edition of the opera based on the Tenbury manuscript, and the German translation of the text included in the score led immediately to a number of German language performances—Munster (1926), Vienna (1927), Stuttgart (1927), and Basle (1931). The score was also used in cities around the world—New York (first staged performance in America: 1932), The Hague (1934), New York (1939), Florence (1940). Dent's edition was the only current publication of the opera until 1960, and thus it must also have been used extensively in the 1950s and 1960s. Britten's version, first performed in 1951, was not commercially available until nine years later.

The edition of Imogen Holst and Benjamin Britten, published by Boosey & Hawkes, uses the Tenbury manuscript, of course, but often decides in favour of readings from the Ohki manuscript, which was used as the primary alternate source. In 1961, Novello & Co. published a new edition edited by Margaret Laurie with a continuo realization by Thurston Dart. Both the Britten/Holst and Laurie editions contain added music for the chorus and dance at the end of Act II; Laurie also prints an overture in G minor that originally may have preceded the Prologue,[2] and she offers suggested settings, based on Purcell's music, for the entire Prologue. Newly composed guitar dances are also supplied. In 1979 the Laurie edition was published without any of the added material as volume 3 of the New Purcell Society Edition, and this was reprinted in 1986 in the Norton Critical Score. In the Purcell Society Edition, the newly discovered Tatton Park manuscript was relied upon as a primary alternate source; Laurie writes in the Preface that 'sometimes, though not always, it seems to give a more accurate rendering [than Tenbury] of the original'.[3] The edition includes a facsimile of the original libretto.

Just as the national premières of *Dido* retell part of the opera's history, so, too, do these editions. They move from corrupt versions based on Academy revisions, to Cummings's reinstatement of lost material, to Dent's edition based on the Tenbury manuscript. After 1950, the editions of Britten/Holst and Laurie lean on rediscovered (Ohki: 1959) or newly discovered (Tatton Park: 1964) manuscripts and both include music for the end of Act II.

My own revision of the Dent edition (1986) relies on the Tenbury manuscript, referring only to the Tatton Park for corroboration of performing details (slurs, figures) and for correction of obvious errors in the Tenbury (missing bars, transposed parts). I have tried to incorporate the research findings reported in this book and have, therefore, preserved the Tenbury metric/tempo markings, included the dance direc-

---

[2] The overture is preserved at the Royal College of Music and entitled 'Overture in Mr P Opera'; see Margaret Laurie, 'Did Purcell set the *Tempest?*', 45, n. 8.

[3] Margaret Laurie, ed. *Dido and Aeneas*, Preface, x.

tions as they appear in the libretto (with indications for their relation to the extant score), offered music of Purcell appropriate for the guitar dances, retained the end of Act II as it stands in the musical sources, and indicated the two-part division of the opera implicit in the Tenbury score as well as the three-act division of the libretto.

3. Recordings

Two versions of *Dido and Aeneas* were recorded before 1950 and released only on 78rpm. (14 sides!). They are no longer available.[4]

Decca X101/7   pre-1936
(US) Decca 25573/9
A Cappella Singers and Boyd Neel String Orchestra
Raybould
N. Evans (Dido), M. Hamlin (Belinda), M. Jarred (Sorceress),
R. Henderson (Aeneas)

HMV C3471/7   pre-1950
Chorus and Philharmonia String Orchestra
C. Lambert
J. Hammond (Dido), I. Baillie (Belinda), E. Coates (Sorceress), D. Noble
(Aeneas), S. Patriss (The Spirit), J. Fullerton (Second Woman), E. Hobson
(First Witch), G. Ripley (Second Witch), T. Jones (Sailor)

In 1952 the first 'modern' recording of *Dido* was released.[5]

Nixa PLP 546   1952
(US) Period PLP 546
Stuart Chamber Chorus and Orchestra
Gregory
E. Houston (Dido), A. Leigh (Belinda), E. Cuthill (Sorceress)
H. Cummings (Aeneas)

At least one American reviewer was less than enthusiastic about the achievement.

> The absurdities of a wretched dramatic confection, jeweled with a compelling music, are not so detractive from musical enjoyment when the work issues from a phonograph and becomes a cantata.... An unusual sensation of intimate participation is possible for the hearer who reproduces this at less than usual volume: the singers become personal and intimate.[6]

---

[4] As listed in *The World's Encyclopedia of Recorded Music*, compiled by Francis F. Clough and G.J. Cuming (London, 1952), 463. (Henceforth, WERM.)
[5] As listed in the Second Supplement (1951–2) of WERM (London, 1953).
[6] C.G. Burke, *High Fidelity*, ii, no. 1 (summer, 1952), 56.

In 1953, the Flagstad performance was released (and reissued in 1969); it includes added music for the end of Act II.[7]

EMI/World Records SH117   1953
Mermaid Theatre Singers and Orchestra
Geraint Jones
K. Flagstad (Dido), E. Schwarzkopf (Belinda), A. Mandikian (Sorceress), T. Helmsley (Aeneas), E. Schwarzkopf (Spirit), E. McNab (Second Woman), S. Rex (First Witch), A. Pollak (Second Witch), D. Lloyd (Sailor)

For the first time *Dido* had received a fully professional performance, and the critics raved.

> At last we have a really satisfactory recording of *Dido*. Bernard Miles describes, in the handsome sleeve-album containing the record, the story of the erection of 'London's only Elizabethan playhouse' and how it was that Kirsten Flagstad came to sing *Dido* in it free and gratis, except for some pints of oatmeal stout following each performance! ... She is, in this recording, in splendid voice and her tone, in her nobly-sung first solo, 'Ah, Belinda,' is most perfectly controlled, her phrasing a joy; and she has evidently, with the humility of a really great artist, studied the word-values with a very good coach. Not once is she tempted to call on anything like the full power of her voice, not even in the dramatic recitative in the scene where Aeneas deserts her. We have had before a record from her of 'When I am laid in earth!' which was good, but now she has grown more into the style and the great lament is nobly done.[8]

In 1962, the Laurie/Dart version was recorded without the added music.

L'Oiseau lyre SOL60047   1962
St. Anthony Singers and the English Chamber Orchestra
Anthony Lewis
J. Baker (Dido), P. Clark (Belinda), M. Sinclair (Sorceress), R. Herincx (Aeneas)

To some minds, Janet Baker's Dido eclipsed Flagstad's interpretation:

> Janet Baker's Dido is the remarkable thing here. Particularly after

---

[7] As listed in WERM Second Supplement. This recording and all following may be found listed also in either *The Illustrated Encyclopedia of Recorded Opera*, by Peter Gammond (New York, 1979), 156–7, or in the 1983 edition of the Gramophone or Schwann catalogues. In all cases only the most recent information available on recording companies and numbers has been provided. Also the dates given are the release dates provided in the Gramophone catalogue. Most of these recordings are reviewed in *The Gramophone* (the journal, not the catalogue), *High Fidelity* and/or *Opera*.

[8] *The Gramophone*, xxx (1953), 204.

fretting for years with the overscaled Flagstad performance, its swoops and scoops, I delight in Miss Baker's purity of line, the delicacy of ornament, the emotion implicit rather than gustily explicit. Above all the sheer beauty of this voice, from the dark, contralto mezza voce ('But death alas I cannot shun') and the white, vibratoless constraint of 'Remember me!', to the gorgeous richness of the voice full-throated, makes this a most memorable performance.[9]

After this point in *Dido*'s history, 'proliferation' is the only word to describe the continued release of new, complete recordings. In 1964, Alfred Deller directed a performance that was largely undistinguished except for the dreadful characterization·of the witches made by having the singers distort their voices.

Vanguard HM46   1964
Oriana Concert Choir and Orchestra
Alfred Deller
M. Thomas (Dido), Sheppard (Belinda), Watts (Sorceress), Bevan (Aeneas)

A pair of interesting recordings appeared in 1965 and 1968. Both use highly esteemed operatic stars in the role of Dido (De los Angeles and Troyanos respectively); both are based on an unpublished edition by Neville D. Boyling that depends on the Tatton Park manuscript; and both include sound effects at the end of the cave scene (thunder and howling wind). In the Troyanos recording, Boyling has arranged music by Purcell for the Act II additions and for the guitar dances. The guitar is also used quite nicely as one of the continuo instruments. In the Troyanos recording 'Ah, Belinda' is performed as it was printed with ornamentation in *Orpheus Britannicus* of 1698 (see Plate 8).

CFP40359 (4) TC CFP40369 (Classics for Pleasure)   1965 (reissued 1981)
(US) Angel S-36359
Ambrosian Singers and the English Chamber Orchestra
Sir John Barbirolli
De los Angeles (Dido), Harper (Belinda), Johnson (Sorceress),
Glossop (Aeneas)

DG 2547 (4) 3347 032 (Deutsche Grammophon)   1968 (reissued 1980)
Hamburg Monteverdi Choir and NDR Chamber Orchestra
Charles Mackerras
Troyanos (Dido), Armstrong (Belinda), Johnson (Sorceress),
McDaniel (Aeneas)

In 1970 a little known recording appeared that seems to have depended on the Laurie edition; it is often quite lovely.

[9] Edward Greenfield, *The Musical Times*, ciii (1962), 329.

Philips 6500 131   1970
John Alldis Choir and the Academy of St-Martin-in-the-Fields
Colin Davis
Veasey (Dido), Donath (Belinda), Bainbridge (Sorceress),
Shirley-Quirk (Aeneas)

In 1977 and 1978 two of the operatic stars who had previously
recorded the role of Dido appeared in second recordings. In neither case
is the second effort as good as the first.

Erato STU71091   1977
(US) RCA ARLI 3021
English Chamber Choir and Orchestra
Raymond Leppard
Troyanos (Dido), Palmer (Belinda), Kern (Sorceress), Stilwell (Aeneas)

Decca SET615   1978
(US) London OSA1170
London Opera Chorus and Aldeburgh Festival Strings
Stuart Bedford
Baker (Dido), Burrowes (Belinda), Reynolds (Sorceress), Pears (Aeneas)

The Janet Baker recording uses the Britten/Holst edition with the
additions at the end of Act II.

There have been two recent recordings that attempt to recreate
Baroque performing practices and perhaps performances closer to
Purcell's original conception. The recordings are strikingly different.

Harmonia Mundi HM10067   1980
Boston Camerata
Joel Cohen
Fortunato (Dido), Armstrong (Belinda), Fithian (Sorceress), M. Baker
(Aeneas)

Chandos ABRD 1034   1981
Taverner Choir and Players
Andrew Parrott
E. Kirkby (Dido), J. Nelson (Belinda), J. Noorman (Sorceress), D. Thomas
(Aeneas)

The Harmonia Mundi recording uses Baroque instruments, and the
orchestra here contains flute and oboe to double the strings and
sometimes play solo lines (as in the Ritornelle in Act II). There is also an
improvised percussion part. Although such instrumental additions can
be verified as an authentic part of Baroque performing practice, the
Tenbury score clearly indicates the use of strings only. The added winds
in this recording can therefore be connected to the corrupt (and certainly
more fulsome) orchestral additions of the eighteenth and nineteenth

centuries. This version gives the role of the Sorceress to a tenor, a choice which, I believe, has no historical justification.

The Chandos recording uses a good combination of instruments to realize the continuo—harpsichord, archlute, and guitar. The style of singing, however, is what distinguishes this version from the others, for Emma Kirkby, Judith Nelson, and David Thomas are consummate masters of Baroque style. The recording is unique for having the sailor sung by a soprano voice (R. Bevan), undoubtedly because the best manuscripts give this role in treble clef. Unfortunately, the Sorceress and the witches are again characterized by voice distortion, instead of allowing Purcell's music to speak for itself.

The most recent recordings add little new to the performance history of *Dido and Aeneas*.[10]

> Teldec 6. 42919AZ   1983
> Arnold-Schönberg-Chor
> Concentus musicus Wien
> Nikolaus Harnoncourt
> A. Murray (Dido), R. Yaker (Belinda), T. Schmidt (Sorceress), A. Scharinger (Aeneas)
>
> Philips 416 299–1   1986
> English Chamber Orchestra
> Raymond Leppard
> J. Norman (Dido), M. McLaughlin (Belinda), P. Kern (Sorceress), T. Allen (Aeneas)

Superficially the recordings are very different. Harnoncourt conducts original instruments and uses relatively unknown soloists with light, clear voices. Leppard uses modern instruments and heavier, operatic voices. Indeed, Jessye Norman's Dido is beautifully sung in the tradition of Kirsten Flagstad. Beyond this, however, the recordings are alike in that neither adds any of the music apparently lacking in Tenbury, and both suffer from similar faults. In particular, very slow tempos frequently disrupt the rhythmic continuity of the opera, and this is compounded by the total separation of movements, such as occurred in the eighteenth-century adaptations. Harnoncourt further emphasizes this separation with exaggerated retardandos on final bars. Both recordings also use quite variable tempos within movements, especially those considered recitative. Not only do both Sorceresses distort their voices, as seems to have become standard, but in the Leppard recording the Sailor and the chorus that repeats the Sailor's song sing with a Cockney accent, which might be considered odd for Trojan sailors. Since each

---

[10] Yet another recording has recently come to my attention, performed by Les Arts Florissants Vocal and Instrumental Ensemble and conducted by William Christie (Harmonia Mundi HMC 5173).

character is clearly defined in his or her music, vocal mannerisms such as these simply hinder a true appreciation of Purcell's acheivement.

Although it still has not appeared at the major operatic houses of the world (such as Covent Garden, La Scala, or the Metropolitan), *Dido and Aeneas* has today found a secure niche in the current operatic repertoire. Its chamber size and fragile melodic and dramatic structure are probably better suited to the small festival houses where it is a regular attraction (Staffordshire, 1957 and 1958, Aix-en-Provence, 1961, and Glynde-bourne, 1966). The opera has and will always be embraced by amateur and school groups; and many of this century's outstanding singers have recorded the opera, which has had at least thirteen complete recordings. In the one hundred years since its modern revival, the growing audience for the opera has left little worry that *Dido and Aeneas* will ever again be lost to the public as it was throughout most of the eighteenth and nineteenth centuries.

Bibliography

Primary Sources

Musical

Dido and Aeneas: scores

Tenbury 1266 (St Michael's College, Tenbury Wells; now housed at Bodleian Library, Oxford), *c.*1775

Tatton Park (Library at Tatton Park, Knutsford, Cheshire; property of National Trust), copied by Philip Hayes, 1784

Ohki (owned and housed by the Nanki Music Library, Tokyo, Japan), *c.*1810

BL Add. MS31450 (British Library, London), perhaps copied by J. P. Hobler, 1784

BL Add. MS15979 (British Library, London), copied by Edward W. Smith, probably from BL Add. MS31450, *c.*1790

Folger F 770 (Folger Shakespeare Library, Washington, DC), late eighteenth century

Dido and Aeneas: parts

RAM 25: (Royal Academy of Music, London) various sets of parts (A–E) dating from the late eighteenth century (A, D), early nineteenth century (C), late nineteenth century (E; with flutes, bassoons, and timpani), and unknown (B: simply a transcription of 'Ah, my Anna' for voice and harpsichord)

Literary

Dido and Aeneas: librettos

[1689]: Chelsea, Josiah Priest's Boarding School for Girls (Royal College of Music, Parry Room Library)

1700: London, Charles Gildon's adaptation of Shakespeare's *Measure for Measure* (British Library: 841 *c.*6)

1774: London, Academy of Ancient Music (New York Public Library)

1787: London, Academy of Ancient Music (Royal College of Music, Portraits' Gallery)

Brutus of Alba

1678: London, printed for Jacob Tonson, *Brutus of Alba: or, the Enchanted Lovers* (Regenstein Library, University of Chicago, Special Collections)

Secondary Sources

Editions

Dido and Aeneas

1841: G. Alexander Macfarren (London: Musical Antiquarian Society, Chappell) full score

1870: Edward Francis Rimbault (for the Musical Antiquarian Society) vocal score, based on Macfarren

1888: William H. Cummings (London: Novello's original octavo edition)

1889: William H. Cummings (London: Purcell Society Edition, Novello) full score printed with 1689 libretto (reprinted by Broude Bros. in 1942)

1924: Artur Bodansky (orchestrator), Gustav Blasser (vocal score) (Vienna: Wiener Philharmonischer Verlag) based on Macfarren

1925: Edward J. Dent (London: Oxford University Press)

1960: Benjamin Britten and Imogen Holst (London: Boosey & Hawkes)

1961: Margaret Laurie and Thurston Dart (London: Novello & Co., Ltd.)

1979: Margaret Laurie (London: New Purcell Society Edition, Novello); reprinted in the Norton Critical Score (1986), see below under Price

1987: Ellen T. Harris (Oxford: Oxford University Press and Eulenburg) revision of Dent

Other:

Dryden, John. *All for Love*, ed. David M. Vieth (London: Edward Arnold Ltd, 1973)

Lawes, William. *Trois Masques à la Cour de Charles Ier d'Angleterre*, ed. Murray Lefkowitz (Paris: Éditions du Centre National de la Recherche Scientifiques, 1970)

Virgil. *Aeneid*, trans. C. Day Lewis (London: Oxford University Press, 1952)

Books and Articles

Arundell, Dennis. *The Critic at the Opera* (London: Benn, 1957/New York: Da Capo, 1980)

—,*Henry Purcell* (Freeport, NY: Books for Libraries Press, 1970)

Balston, Thomas. *James Whatman, Father and Son* (London: Methuen, 1957)

Bukofzer, Manfred. *Music in the Baroque Era* (New York: W.W. Norton & Co., 1947)

Burney, Charles. *A General History of Music from the Earliest Ages to the*

Present Period (1789), ed. Frank Mercer (New York: Harcourt, Brace, and Co., 1957)

Buttrey, John. 'Dating Purcell's *Dido and Aeneas*', *Proceedings of the Royal Music Association*, civ (1967–8), 51–62

Chan, Mary. 'The Witch of Endor and Seventeenth-Century Propaganda', *Musica Disciplina*, 34 (1980), 205–14

Charteris, Richard. 'Some Manuscript Discoveries of Henry Purcell and his Contemporaries in the Newberry Library, Chicago', *Musical Library Association Notes*, 37 (1980), 7–13

Craven, Robert R. 'Nahum Tate's Third *Dido and Aeneas*: The Sources of the Libretto to Purcell's Opera', *The World of Opera*, 1 (1979), 65–78

Cummings, William H. 'Dido and Aeneas', *The Musical Times*, li (1910), 363–64

—,*Henry Purcell* (London: S. Low, Marston, Searle & Revington, 1881)

Dent, Edward J. *The Foundations of English Opera* (Cambridge: Cambridge University Press, 1928/ New York: Da Capo, 1965)

Dryden, John. *Essays of John Dryden*, ed. W. P. Ker (Oxford: Oxford University Press, 1926)

Duckles, Vincent and Franklin B. Zimmerman. *Words to Music: Papers on English Seventeenth-Century Song* (Los Angeles: William Andrews Clark Memorial Library, 1967)

Dupre, Henry. *Purcell* (Paris: F. Alcan, 1927)

Fortune, Nigel. 'A New Purcell Source', *Music Review*, xxv (1964), 109–13

Grattan Flood, W. H. 'Purcell's *Dido and Aeneas*: Who was Lady Dorothy Burke?', *The Musical Times*, liv (1918), 515

Harley, John. *Music in Purcell's London: The Social Background* (London: Dobson, 1968)

Harris, Ellen T. *Handel and the Pastoral Tradition* (London: Oxford University Press, 1980)

—,'Recitative and Aria in *Dido and Aeneas*', *Studies in the History of Music*, ii (1987)

Hawkins, Sir John. *A General History of the Science and Practice of Music* (London: Novello, Elver & Co., 1875/orig. 1776)

Haun, Eugene. *But Hark! More Harmony: The Libretti of Restoration Opera in English* (Ypsilanti, Mich.: Eastern Michigan University Press, 1971)

Holland, Arthur Keith. *Henry Purcell: the English Musical Tradition* (Freeport, NY: Books for Libraries Press, 1970)

Holst, Gustav. 'Henry Purcell: 1658–1695', *The Heritage of Music*, ed. Hubert J. Foss (London: Oxford University Press, 1927)

Holst, Imogen, ed., *Henry Purcell (1659–1695): Essays on his Music* (London: Oxford University Press, 1959)

—,*Henry Purcell: the Story of his Life and Work* (London: Boosey & Hawkes, 1961)

Hudson, Frederick. 'The Earliest Paper Made by James Whatman the Elder (1702–1759) and its Significance in Relation to G. F. Handel and John Walsh', *The Music Review*, xxxvlii (1977), 15–32

Kerman, Joseph. *Opera as Drama* (New York: Knopf, 1956), 56–61

Laurie, Margaret. 'Did Purcell set the *Tempest?*', *Proceedings of the Royal Music Association*, xc (1963–4), 43–57

—,'Purcell's Stage Works' (Unpublished Ph.D. dissertation: Cambridge University, 1962)

Lewis, Anthony. *The Language of Purcell: National Idiom or Local Dialect?* (A Ferens Inaugual Lecture: University of Hull, 1968)

Mellers, Wilfrid. 'The Tragic Heroine and the Un-Hero; Henry Purcell: *Dido and Aeneas*', in *Harmonius Meeting: a Study of the Relationship between English Music, Poetry and Theatre*, *c.*1600-1900 (London: Denis Dobson, 1965), 203–14

Moore, Robert Etheridge. *Henry Purcell and the Restoration Theatre* (Cambridge, Mass.: Harvard University Press, 1961)

North, Roger. *Memoirs of Music*, ed. Edward F. Rimbault (London, 1846)

—,*Roger North on Music*, ed. John Wilson (London: Novello, 1959)

Porter, Andrew. 'Musical Events: British Worthy', *The New Yorker*, 55 (7 May 1979), 144–7

Price, Curtis A. *Music in the Restoration Theatre* (Ann Arbor: UMI, 1979)

—,*Henry Purcell and the London Stage* (Cambridge: Cambridge University Press, 1984)

—,*Henry Purcell, 'Dido and Aeneas': An Opera* (New York: W. W. Norton & Co., 1986

—,and Irena Cholij. 'Dido's Bass Sorceress', *The Musical Times*, cxxvii (1986), 615–18

Radice, Mark. 'Tate's libretto for *Dido and Aeneas*: a Revaluation', *Bach: The Quarterly Journal of the Riemenschneider-Bach Institute*, vii (January 1976), 20–26

Rohrer, Katherine. 'The Energy of English Words: Text and Expression in Purcell's Vocal Music' (Unpublished Ph.D. dissertation: Princeton University, 1980)

Savage, Roger. 'Producing *Dido and Aeneas*: An Investigation into Sixteen Problems', *Early Music*, iv (1976), 393–406

Sietz, Reinhold. *Henry Purcell: Zeit, Leben, Werk* (Leipzig: Breitkopf & Härtel, 1955)

Spencer, Christopher. *Nahum Tate* (New York: Twayne Publishers, 1972)

Spink, Ian. *English Song: Dowland to Purcell* (London: Batsford, 1974)

Squire, W. Barclay. 'Purcell's *Dido and Aeneas*', *The Musical Times*, liv (1918), 252–4

Westrup, Jack A. *Purcell* (London: J.M. Dent & Sons, Ltd., 1947; first published 1936)

White, Eric Walter. 'English Opera Research -The Immediate Past and the Future: A Personal Viewpoint', *Theatre Notebook*, xxi (1966), 32–7

—,*A History of English Opera* (London: Faber and Faber, 1983)

Zimmerman, Franklin B. *Henry Purcell (1659–1695): His Life and Times* (2nd rev. edn. Philadelphia: University of Pennsylvania, 1983)

—,*Henry Purcell (1659–1695): An Analytical Catalogue of his Music* (London: Macmillan, 1963)

—,*Henry Purcell (1659–1695): Melodic and Intervallic Indexes to his Complete Works* (Philadelphia: Smith-Edward-Dunlap, 1971)

References to Individual Movements in *Dido and Aeneas*

References to movements are given wherever the text or music is discussed regardless of whether the movement title is actually mentioned. For example, 'When I am laid in earth' is frequently referred to as Dido's lament, and 'Stay, Prince, and hear' as Aeneas's monologue. See also the plot summaries, pp. 12–14 and 70–3, Table 1 (p. 77), and Table 2 (pp. 99–100). References to musical examples are given in italics. The movements are given in order following the numeration in the author's edition of *Dido and Aeneas* (Oxford and Eulenburg).

1. Shake the cloud 37–8, 39, 70, 99, *138*, Plate 5
2. Banish sorrow 66, 70–1, 99, 112, *140*, Plate 5
3. Ah! Belinda 29, 70, 71, 97, *98*, 99, 107, *108, 109, 110, 111*, 112–13, 115 n., 116, 128 n., 128–9, 133, *137, 138, 140*, 169–70
4. Grief increases by concealing 54, 70, 97, 99, 133, *135*, Plate 5
5. When monarchs unite 39, 66, 70, 76, 99, *135*, Plate 5
6. Whence could so much virtue spring 38, 40, 53–5, 70, 93, *94–5, 95–6*, 99, 101, 103, *136, 137*, 144, 145 n.
7/8. Fear no danger to ensue 40, 64, 66, 71, 76, 99, 125
9. See, your royal guest appears 39, 49, 71, 74, 98–9
10. Cupid only throws the dart 40, 66, 71, 74, 99, *139*
11. If not for mine 40, 71, 77, 99, 133
12. Pursue thy conquest, Love 40, 67, 71, 74, 78, 99, 133, *139*, 160
13. A Dance Gittars Chacony 64, 67, 71, 167–8, 170
14. To the hills and the vales 12, 71, 78, 99
15. The Triumphing Dance 46, 64, 66, 71, 107, 112–13, 116, 128–9
16. Wayward sisters 40, 71, 100, 128 n., 128–9
17. Harm's our delight 50, 52, 66, 71, 100
18. The Queen of Carthage 21, 41, 71, 78, 100
19/21. Ho, ho, ho 53, 66, 71, 100, *134*
20. Ruin'd ere the set of sun? 52, 100
22. But ere we this perform 21, 65–6, 72, 100, *134*
23. In our deep vaulted cell 40, 72, 78, 100, 128 n.
24. Echo Dance of Furies 13, 55, 64, 66–7, *67*, 72, *80*, 107, 128
25/33. Ritornelle 72, 79–80, *80*, 171
26/27. Thanks to these lonesome vales 26, 50–1, 52, 64–6, 68, 72, 100
28. Gitter ground a Dance 64, 67, 72, 167–8, 170

Index

References to musical examples are given in italics. Musical works are listed under composer and librettist, literary works under the author. Titles are indexed only of works important to the discussion with cross-references to the author(s). Cross-references are also given in all cases where an alternate entry is deemed complementary or especially useful. A separate index of individual movements in *Dido and Aeneas* is on p. 179.

Academy of Ancient Music 46, 123–6, 146
Ádám, Jenö 160, 165
Aeneas, character of 14–17, 27–8, 32, 70–4, 76, 98, 145 (*see also* Dido, Purcell, Tate)
Aeneid (*see* Virgil)
Anne, Queen 60
antimasque 84 (*see also* masque)
Aristotle 41, 42 n. (*see also* Tate)
Arne, Thomas 146
Arnold, Dr Samuel 125

Bach, Johann Sebastian 107, 152–3
Bach Choir 150
Baker, Dame Janet 163, 166, 169–71
Beaumont, Sir Francis 82
Beethoven, Ludwig van 107
Belinda (*see* Tenbury ms.)
Blasser, Gustav 157
Blow, John 95, 97, 101, 106; *Venus and Adonis* 7–8, 31, 70, 74–5, 89, *92*, 93, 99 n.
Bodansky, Artur 157–60, 165–6
Boyce, William 146
Boyling, Neville 170
Britten, Benjamin 161–4, 166–7, 171
Bukofzer, Manfred 105–6
Burke, Lady Dorothy 5, 33
Busenello, Giovanni, *La Didone* 29–30
Buttrey, John 5–6, 17–19, 31

Carissimi, Giacomo 101; *Jepthe* 103, *104*, 105
Cavalli, Francesco, *La Didone* 29, 104
Charles I 8, 18
Charles II 31
Cholij, Irena 63 n.

Cokain, Aston 34
Comus (*see* Henry Lawes)
Concerts of Ancient Music 123–5, 148, 150
Cooke, Captain 36, 88
Cummings, William 130, 148–50, 160, 166–7
Cupid and Death (*see* Locke)

dance song 87 (*see* tuneful air)
Dart, Thurston 167, 169
Davenant, William 88–9; *Gondibert* 36, 89; *Macbeth* 22; *The Siege of Rhodes* 88–9; *The Tempest* 55
declamatory air 85–90, 92–5, 97–100, 106; compared to continental recitative 85, 88, 91, 96–7, 101–6, 135, 144–6, 154
De los Angeles, Victoria 170
Dent, Edward 160–1, 165–7
Desmarets, Henri, *Didon* 30
dialogue 85, 89, 97–8, 100
Dido, character of 11–17, 22–7, 70–1, 74, 76, 78, 112, 117; death of 11–12, 14–17, 19, 22–5, 29–31, 39, 56, 73, 118–19 (*see also* Aeneas, Purcell, Tate)
Donne, John 119
dramatic opera 6, 8–10, 55, 59
Dryden, John 6–8, 35–7, 89; *Albion and Albanius* 35, 37–8, 58; *All for Love* 27–9, 35, 41; *The Indian Queen* 7; *King Arthur* 7, 58; *The State of Innocence* 35; *The Tempest* 55
D'Urfey, Thomas 5, 33

Eccles, John, *Mars and Venus* 48 n., 61–3
Elizabeth I 19
Etherege, George, *The Man of Mode* 48 n.
Evelyn, John 89